CE

JOSEPH L. BRISTOW:

Kansas Progressive

JOSEPH L. BRISTOW:

Kansas Progressive

A. Bower Sageser

THE UNIVERSITY PRESS OF KANSAS
Lawrence and London

To my wife, Ruth, and to my daughter, Sandra Jean, who in her undergraduate major chose to follow in the footsteps of her father.

Preface

The nineteenth- and early twentieth-century political liberals were strong believers in institutional perfectibility and equalitarianism. Their reforming zeal was devoted to broadening democracy and to improvements in the techniques of governmental administration. Men from all backgrounds joined the march for progress, and many editors and journalists were among the new recruits. Joseph Little Bristow, an influential Kansas newspaper editor, was closely identified with the new and exciting era of American political life. The story of this Kansas liberal and his contributions to state and national politics deserves study.

After graduation from Baker University in 1886, Bristow served two terms as clerk of the district court in Douglas County. In 1890 he purchased the Salina *Daily Republican,* and he later owned and edited several other newspapers in Kansas. In his role as editor, he supported many of the liberal issues of the day.

Bristow was a leader among the Republicans in Kansas, serving as a private secretary to Governor Edmund N. Morrill and as secretary to the state central committee of the Republican party. After the election of President William McKinley in 1896, Bristow became fourth assistant postmaster-general, a position he held until 1905. During these years in Washington, he won a national reputation for the investigation of frauds in the postal service. He broke with President Roosevelt in 1905 and for a short time served as a trouble-shooter in the Panama Canal Zone for William H. Taft.

From 1909 to 1915, Bristow was in the United States Senate, gaining a reputation as one of the hardest workers among the insurgent senators, and for three years he was a member of the Kansas Utilities Commission.

Throughout his public and editorial career Bristow was most effective in securing the adoption of progressive reforms, at both state and national levels.

The main source for this study was the Bristow Papers at the Kansas State Historical Society. For a broader understanding of the man, many other public and private papers were examined, including those of Albert B. Cummins, Albert J. Beveridge, Jonathan P. Dolliver, George Norris, William Allen White, Arthur Capper, Chester I. Long, William H. Taft, and Theodore Roosevelt.

Many helped to make this study possible. Homer E. Socolofsky found valuable letters in Capper's papers, which he made available to me. Some financial support was given by the Bureau of General Research at Kansas State University. Nyle Miller and his staff at the Kansas State Historical Society were always ready to assist, as were the custodians of the other collections in which I worked. My wife, Ruth, typed the first draft, and the final draft was typed by Marilyn Sullivan and Jean Paquette. These and many others helped to complete the study of *Joseph L. Bristow: Kansas Progressive.*

• Contents •

ILLUSTRATIONS

The Beginnings and the Man

Joseph Little Bristow was born near Hazel Green, Wolfe County, Kentucky, on July 22, 1861, the day after Union troops suffered a bitter defeat in the first battle of Bull Run. Union feeling in Kentucky was strong, and many Kentucky boys were enlisting in the northern army. L. G. Olmstead of New York had proposed a new *Book of Martyrs,* soliciting authentic information on "every case of outrage and wrong perpetuated by the Southern chivalry upon the Northern citizens and upon Southern men who have suffered on account of anti-slavery principles," in order to put them on record for the information of future generations.[1]

Bristow had no later recollection of the log cabin in which he was born, and he was too young to remember the war. His father enlisted in Company K, 24th Kentucky Volunteer Infantry, on September 29, 1861,[2] and his mother moved to another section of the state to be free from Confederate raiders. Much of Bristow's early life was spent on a farm, and he was surrounded by deep religious influences: both his grandfather and his father were Methodist circuit riders. He grew to manhood during the post-war period, filled with stories of the Civil War and Republican patriotism. He had nearly completed his college career before he saw a Democrat President of the United States.

The young Kentuckian came of well-established American stock. He was of the seventh generation descended from John Bristow, who came from Bristol, England, and settled in Middlesex County in Virginia during the 1680's. There on the Rappahannock River the first Bristow acquired lands, some of which were still in the family's name in 1900. John Bristow returned to die in England about 1767,[3] but other members of the Bristow family moved westward, and there were Bristows in eastern Kentucky nearly a century before Joseph was born. His grandfather, Joseph H. Bristow, was born in Kentucky and died in Baldwin, Kansas, in 1896. William Bristow, Joseph's father, was born in Montgomery County, Kentucky, in 1837. He was educated in the Bath County schools, and in 1858 he married Savannah Little, a Kentucky girl with Virginia ancestry. Two children were born to this couple, Sarah Ann in 1859 and Joseph Little.[4]

After serving three years and four months in the Union army, William became a teacher, a preacher for the Kentucky Methodist Conference, and a farmer. When his wife died in 1868, his children moved to the home of his parents, and in 1871, William was transferred to the Kansas Methodist Conference at Fredonia. In May, 1871, he married a schoolteacher, Ellen Longwell, and during this second marriage two boys and two girls were added to the family.[5] In 1873 young Joseph and his sister, Sarah, joined their father in Kansas.

William was a thorough pioneer organizer and builder, serving several churches and starting Sunday schools and teachers' institutes. He was superannuated in the early 1880's and moved to Baldwin, Kansas, where he operated a hardware store. He was a frank, outspoken man, intolerant of wrongdoing, and incorruptible. Joseph was deeply influenced by his father, who kept up a steady correspondence with his son, often running political errands for him until his death on March 16, 1921.

Joseph Bristow was eleven years old when he first set foot on Kansas soil. He attended school for about three years but developed no great liking for study. He grew restless and homesick, and when he was fourteen, he returned to Kentucky to live with his grandfather and an uncle. His grandfather had given up riding the Methodist circuit and was farming. The two men, according to Bristow, were "kind hearted and indulgent"; they allowed him to stay away from school and spend his time on the farm or hunting and fishing. "I was ignorant, of course and unsophisticated, but happily, I was not without sentiment," he declared in an interview with James B. Murrow in 1909.[6] Joseph remained in Kentucky until he was eighteen. At that time he stood six feet, two and one-half inches. He was skinny but could take his place as a full hand in the harvest or at the plow.

During this stay in Kentucky, he met and courted Margaret Hester Hendrix, an orphan who lived with her brother on a farm in Fleming County. The couple was married at Flemingsburg on November 12, 1879. In later years Bristow declared that he was, at the time of his marriage, "old enough" to comprehend the responsibilities of matrimony and to understand the "limitations" of Kentucky. Soon after the wedding the young bride and bridegroom departed for his father's home at Howard City in Elk County, Kansas, making the trip by train to Eureka and by stagecoach some thirty miles to the parsonage home of the Reverend William Bristow. It was quite a shock for all when Joseph introduced his bride to his father and stepmother, and Joseph later declared that his father never appeared so tall as then.[7]

Joseph went to work at once. He shocked corn during the fall and winter for $2.25 a day. He was fortunate in finding a settler who felt crowded because he had a neighbor one-half mile away; for the sum of $300 and the assumption of a $250 mortgage, the settler sold his equity in an eighty-acre pre-emption claim to the Bristows. The farm was in the Flint Hills, about ten miles from Howard City. There in a one-room log cabin, with furniture made of dry-goods boxes, the Bristows started their career as pioneer farmers. Their front yard reached to Canada and the back yard was lapped by the waters of the Gulf of Mexico. A few head of cattle and horses were purchased, and the land, which had been broken by the previous settler, was farmed.

Farming in Kansas was a new and difficult experience for the bride. As soon as they moved into their cabin, Joe went to the timbered area along the banks of Elk Creek, about three miles from the cabin, to cut fence posts. On the first day Maggie became frightened by a high wind, and the second day brought a crisis when smoke and ashes blew in from the northern rim of the horizon, from a prairie fire, turning the noon into near-twilight. When Joe returned home, he was greeted by a bride in tears; she was certain she would never like Kansas and urged her husband to take her back to Kentucky. New arrangements had to be made. On the next day Joe took Maggie with him to the creek. He fixed a fishline and hook, and Maggie caught all the bass they could eat that day. The neighbors had given them a dog, which became an established member of the family, and Maggie soon learned to enjoy life on the farm, in spite of considerable poverty. She liked to ride a horse and rode as well as Joe. Having grown up on farms, both the Bristows loved the land, and throughout most of their married life they owned farm land.

Like many of his young contemporaries who later entered politics, Bristow became interested in a debating club during his stay on the farm, and it strongly affected his future career. In the local literary society Bristow found that he had an interest in subjects other than farming, and he enjoyed argument and debate. Soon he was considering other fields for his life work. He frequently consulted his father, who impressed upon his son that he could do little without an education. This counseling and encouragement from his father led Bristow to seek a college education in which he would train for the ministry. After eighteen months and two crops, the Bristows sold the farm, having accumulated some $1,600 in money and property.[8] Their first son had been born in 1880, and the family now moved to Baldwin, where Joseph entered the preparatory department of Baker University in 1881.

The family moved into two rooms and remained in Baldwin until Joseph completed his work for the A.B. degree, graduating with honors in 1886. Their funds were meager, and Joseph did many kinds of work to finance his education. In the summers he walked from farm to farm and from town to town selling books, and incidentally obtaining many new points of view on human nature. One winter he had to choose between purchasing an overcoat or a Webster's unabridged dictionary; he chose the latter.

Baker University had been founded by a group of Methodists in 1858. The early years were filled with the trials that most private frontier schools experienced. By 1881, when Bristow enrolled, the university was becoming somewhat more prosperous and was enjoying a period of stability, growth, and greater effectiveness under the presidency of William H. Sweet. During Sweet's administration, between 1879 and 1886, the enrollment increased and new buildings were erected.[9] In addition to the traditional classical subjects, Bristow studied advanced mathematics, the physical and biological sciences, and a modest amount of history and government. He participated in the extracurricular affairs of the school, which centered largely in the activities of the literary societies.

There were four main literary societies, meeting weekly, in which members pursued their interests in music, art, oratory, and debate. Bristow was a leader in the Biblical Society, the oldest of the four organizations. The societies sustained a lecture bureau, using outside talent, and edited a monthly campus magazine, the *Baldwin Index.*

These groups offered elementary training in caucuses, parliamentary tactics, debate, and political warfare. In 1883, Baker University celebrated its silver anniversary, and during the celebration the literary societies conducted a full week's program. Henry W. Mayo and Bristow were the main debaters, and Edwin M. Randall and William A. Quayle were the principal orators.[10] Quayle, who later became a bishop in the Methodist church, was one of Bristow's closest friends. While in the United States Senate, Bristow purchased the fire-proof cases that now house the Quayle Bible Collection in the library at Baker University.

During his senior year Bristow edited a review section for the *Baldwin Index.* Here he included brief notices of books and articles from many magazines, on history, art, literature, poetry, education, and science. His dry humor is shown in an entry in which he wrote, "Quite a number of the reviews are not original, but probably they are almost as good as if I had written them."[11] Had the editor examined all the books and articles reviewed, he would, indeed, have been a well-read man. For the June, 1886, issue of the *Index,* Bristow wrote an original article, entitled "The Two Republics." It was a comparative study of the governments of France and the United States. The young author expressed his belief that good "moral principles" had helped to make the American system the stronger of the two.

The contributions to the *Index* were only a part of Bristow's journalistic experience as a college student. On occasion he wrote anonymous letters to local editors encouraging reforms in the management of local civic affairs. For a short time, in 1885, he owned and edited a newspaper. Bristow and J. Leeford Brady bought the *Visitor* and the *Criterion,* two small weekly papers, and combined them into the Baldwin *Ledger.* The editors hoped to give the southern section of Douglas County a strong Republican press, "as we everyday become more convinced that the prosperity of our country depends on the principles of the Republican Party."[12] Bristow borrowed money and purchased Brady's interest, and within a few months he sold the *Ledger* to Dr. D. W. Scott. In his final editorial Bristow stated that he had tried to give the community a Republican and prohibitionist press.[13] He claimed later that he had made about $300 on the newspaper consolidation and sale.[14] Whatever his financial gains, these editorial ventures started Joseph Bristow on the career of a newspaper man, and soon after entering public life he became owner of several newspapers in the state. For over thirty-five years he was to be owner and editor of a Kansas newspaper.

In 1908, Frank C. Lockwood wrote, "The education secured in a Kansas college a quarter of a century ago was a crude and anomalous possession, but such as it was young Bristow got it; and it has done him no harm." Lockwood felt that Bristow's training in college politics, together with his experience in public speaking, contributed to his later successful public career.[15] There were deeper and more lasting influences. Bristow learned the economic and cultural values of a college education and tried hard to impress these values on his sons. He developed an interest in history, government, and literature and continued to read them extensively throughout his life. His editorials and speeches reflected a sound historical background, though, at times he was guilty of overusing historical precedents. He learned to be independent in his thinking and thorough in his research for the truth.

Bristow continually supported the cause of education, and his support of the progressive movement was bolstered by his belief that political liberalism would come to the United States only as the people became educated. He kept in close touch with his alma mater, making modest financial contributions and serving on the Board of Trustees from 1905 to 1944. He corresponded frequently with the board members and with the president of Baker, occasionally recommending candidates for teaching positions. On one occasion he wrote an effective letter urging the reinstatement of football at Baker University, in which he pointed out the merits of the game, the value of rugged competition, and the influence of an occasional defeat upon the college student.[16] In later years, when he lived at Ossian Hall in Virginia, he made two annual pilgrimages to Kansas: one for election day and one for the meeting of the Board of Trustees at Baker. He received an M.A. degree from Baker in 1889, and in 1909 the university awarded him an honorary LL.D. degree. During his residence in Salina he also served on the Board of Trustees at Salina Wesleyan University.

In 1881, Bristow had entered Baker University to study for the ministry. By graduation time, in 1886, he had concluded somehow that he had "not been called." This worried him considerably. An old friend of the family advised him that unless he really felt "the call" he should seek employment elsewhere.[17] No doubt the church lost a minister with promise, but politics gained a courageous and energetic leader.

Bristow had considered journalism, law, and politics as possible careers. In 1884 he had organized a Blaine-Logan club at

Baker and enlisted fifty-one out of fifty-two voters in the university under his banner. He first planned to seek a seat in the state legislature, but on the advice of the Douglas County sheriff he decided to be a candidate for clerk of the district court instead. With the help of the old-timers, the southern part of Douglas County was lined up for the young university graduate. On September 4, 1886, the editor of the Baldwin *Ledger* announced that Palmyra Township would present to the Republican county convention the "solitary" name of Joseph L. Bristow as a candidate for clerk of the district court. The editor declared that Mr. Bristow was a "very worthy" young man and had "always been a rabid Republican." On September 25, Bristow won the convention vote, defeating his nearest rival by a vote of eighty-four to fifty-four. Bristow rented a horse and buggy for $1.25 a day (payment sometime in the future) and proceeded to conduct a vigorous personal campaign. He won his first elective contest in November by a seven hundred majority. The Baldwin *Ledger* heralded his victory: "Rah for our Joe—The Next Clerk of the Court." The editor declared, "Our Joseph is on his pegs, high in the air and says it is all clear up to there now." With the local band the people gave the new clerk of the court a "jolly ratification." The editor concluded that the seven hundred majority "makes the boy sleep well."[18]

The election victory brought joy to the Bristow family. They had lived on very little for five years in order that the father could obtain a college degree. During that time the family had grown.[19] There were college debts to be paid, and there were unpaid campaign expenses. The clerkship of the court, while not paying a high salary, would provide a steady income for the growing family. Furthermore, Joseph could read and study law under a competent lawyer when the Bristows moved to Lawrence.

There are few measuring sticks for the successful conduct of the position of clerk of the court. What evidence there is shows that Bristow conducted his work in an efficient manner, and he was easily re-elected in the Republican landslide of 1888. During his four years in office, Bristow read law and continued his Republican party activities. He became president of the Young Men's Republican Club at Lawrence, and he campaigned throughout the state for Benjamin Harrison in 1888. The short distance from Lawrence to Topeka enabled Bristow to become well acquainted with party leaders in the capital. Some were already impressed by the young man's energetic work for the party.

With his law studies nearly completed Bristow turned back to an earlier interest, newspaper work. In September, 1890, he purchased the Salina *Daily Republican.* In writing of the purchase, the editor of the Lawrence *Journal* described Bristow as one of the "most brilliant" young men in the state: "In all his work he is faithful, in all his friendships sincere, in republicanism true to the core, and in private life an accomplished, cultivated and educated gentleman."[20]

Newspapers were "solid gold" investments during this period. By careful management one could easily double the financial value of a newspaper in less than a decade. Bristow purchased the Salina *Journal* in 1893 from C. B. Kirtland and combined it with the *Republican.* He owned and edited the *Republican* until July 2, 1894. That year he started the *Irrigation Farmer* in response to the economic needs of the day.

The early 1890's, when Bristow was an active newspaper editor in Salina, were critical years in the economic and political development of Kansas. It was not easy for the editor to become a molder of public opinion, especially while continuing to espouse the Republican cause, as he did. The deep political and economic unrest was reflected by the fact that in October, 1890, the state had 2,886 Farmers' Alliance organizations with a membership of 140,000. In the election of 1890 the Alliance (or the People's party, as it came to be called) captured five out of seven congressional districts in Kansas and won a total of ninety-two seats in the Kansas House of Representatives. That was the year in which Jerry Simpson had climaxed a speech on capital and the tariff by taking off his boot, pulling up his trousers to his knees—exhibiting a naked foot and leg, and declaring that under the high tariff the Kansas farmer "can't have no drawers, and ain't got no socks."

This featured speech soon won Simpson the nickname of "Sockless Jerry." The prohibition issue was raging.[21] Many women assisted in breaking up the furniture and glass in Kansas saloons, and almost weekly, druggists were arrested by the "buggy load" for the illegal sale of liquor. As a result of the panic conditions, sweeping Populist victories followed the 1890 success and left the shattered major parties groping for leadership and strength after the November election of 1892.

On January 29, 1892, a few Republican leaders, mostly editors, held the first Kansas Day Club banquet in Topeka. The affair, according to reports, was arranged to some extent for social purposes, but the real object was to mobilize party strength. In March the Republican League was formed and Bristow became a member.[22] January and February in 1893 witnessed the "40 Day and 40 Night" legislative war between the elected Republican and Populist forces for the control of the lower house of the Kansas legislature. The Republicans gained control but achieved little in legislative matters.[23] By 1894 there were signs of a fusion between the Democrats and the Populists.[24]

According to the Populist leaders, Kansas was to be the battleground of the nation in the election of 1894. It was predicted that if Kansas could be held, the Populists could win at least eight other states,[25] and many of the best speakers in the party were sent to Kansas during the spring and summer of 1894. During this time Bristow edited one of the few presses in the state that hammered at the Populists—almost to the point of slander—and tried to bring strength to his own party. He frequently ridiculed Mary E. Lease, Jerry Simpson, Senator W. A. Peffer, and Governor L. D. Lewelling. When the editor of the Boston *Herald* described a hypothetical troupe to be made up of the Populists in Kansas, producing a tragedy with Governor Lewelling as the "heavy villain" and Mary Lease as the "avenger," Bristow passed the account on to his readers.[26] And when only three persons remained in the United States Senate to hear Peffer's tariff speech, Bristow compared the "rush-out" to the famous "rush-in" when Senator John J. Ingalls had occupied the Senate floor in the past. He concluded that these were "surely the days of mediocrity" so far as Kansas representation on the floors of Congress was concerned.[27] He chided Peffer for his inactivity, saying it had been a long time since that "modern knight errant, the light and mirror of Machegan chivalry, has tackled a windmill"; Bristow had expected "thrusts" on the Hawaiian question, tariff, or silver. He recorded the progress of Coxey's march and rejoiced over the small number of followers from Kansas. When the march failed, he wrote that it "was now known" as the "Coxey Movement (Limited)."[28]

In later years Bristow declared that his anti-Populist editorials had been costly to him. He lost many of his subscribers, and many of his advertisers left his paper because they feared that the farmers would not buy their goods if they advertised in the *Republican*. But Bristow was not always critical of Populist activities in Washington. He supported Peffer's stand on the income tax issue, as well as his proposal to investigate speculation in the sugar industry. Bristow was remarkably tolerant of President Grover Cleveland's refusal to allow the annexation of Hawaii by the United States. Many of his editorials were written to bring his own party into line on some of the leading questions of the day. He supported the idea of an independent tariff commission, gave more than ample space to the woman suffrage movement, called for income tax and better banking laws, and took special interest in the use of the party primary to select delegates to state conventions.

From 1891 to 1894, Bristow had his eye on a possible congressional seat in the Fifth District. He was active in district party meetings and was a delegate to the state conventions in 1892 and 1894. In April, 1894, he announced his candidacy for nomination as congressman by the Republican party and published a full list of articles written in other newspapers which endorsed him for the position. However, when William A. Calderhead of Marysville, Kansas, got the nod from the Fifth District convention, Bristow readily gave him his support.

Bristow's editorial and political efforts did not go unrewarded. In 1894 he became the secretary for the Republican state central committee, and in July, 1894, he sold the *Republican* in order to give more time to his duties as secretary.[29] Cyrus Leland of Troy, Kansas, was president of the Republican central committee at this time. He was later selected as a member of the Republican National Committee. An influential conservative, he had been appointed a collector of internal revenue in Kansas by President Benjamin Harrison. Leland and Bristow made a powerful team.

As early as March 19, 1894, Bristow had written that William McKinley would be the next occupant of the White House. Leland and Bristow invited McKinley and Thomas B. Reed to campaign in the state. Reed declined, but McKinley came to Kansas in October to help his party recapture the state. McKinley made a one-day tour, speaking in seventeen towns, and according to contemporary accounts, the visit of the "apostle of protection" was a great success.[30] McKinley was impressed with Bristow, whom he met for the first time on this visit; and later, after he had been elected President of the United States, McKinley appointed Bristow fourth assistant postmaster-general.

Bristow was an effective worker during the campaign. He gained recognition by his Kansas Day address, "Why a Young Man Should be a Republican." But the greatest reward came after the party victory in the November election. Governor-elect Edmund N. Morrill, who had been drafted from political retirement to aid the Republicans in their fight for victory, selected Bristow to serve as his private secretary. Bristow held this position for two years.

During these early years in politics, Bristow remained in the newspaper business. Besides publishing the *Irrigation Farmer* he purchased the Ottawa *Herald* in 1895 and kept this financial interest for ten years. His partner in the purchase of the *Herald* was Henry J. Allen, who later owned the Wichita *Beacon*. Allen managed the *Herald,* and in 1903 he and Bristow purchased the Salina *Daily Republican Journal*. Bristow became sole owner in 1907, and the *Journal* remained under his control until 1925.

As an editor and publisher, as a private secretary to the governor, and as the secretary of his party's central committee, Bristow was indeed in the inner council of the Republican party in Kansas. His position as a newspaper man put him in a group of young editors from which the leadership of the Republican party emerged by 1900.[31] Some of these editors were conservative, others were moderate, and a few were extremely liberal. In 1895, Bristow fitted best into the "moderate" classification. It took eight years of political seasoning in Washington, D.C., before Bristow was classified by his contemporaries as a "radical" or an "insurgent." By 1908 many local editors had become the chief contributors to and spokesmen for the national progressive movement as it developed in Kansas, but before then Bristow was exercising his influence on Morrill's administration and on the Republican party.

The Editor and
the Irrigation Crusade

During the 1890's there was great economic and political unrest in the Midwest; it was a period in which a nationwide depression was aggravated by frontier conditions and recurring periods of drought. Joseph Bristow was maturing as a man, as an editor, and as a public figure during these critical years, and the economic forces of the times helped to shape his thinking and to direct his actions.

One movement in which he was especially active, and which cannot be entirely separated from his political activity, was the revival of the great drive to irrigate the semi-arid lands of the Midwest. He took part in local, regional, and national associations designed to champion the cause of irrigation and to seek state and federal assistance for irrigation projects. From February, 1894, to November, 1896, he published the *Irrigation Farmer,* a small monthly journal devoted "wholly to the interest of irrigation for the Great Plains."[1] Its purpose was, according to the editor in the first issue, "to aid the farmer in finding the most practical and profitable way" of irrigating his farm and to give "him the information necessary for success."

One of Bristow's critics wrote in 1894 that Joe was trying to "sail into Congress" on the irrigation issue but "was grounded on a sand bar" in 1894 when he lost his party's nomination to Congress. A supporter at the same time declared that if "Bristow will continue his 'irrigation racket' he will be of more service to his country than two-thirds of all the Congressmen that ever lived."[2] Bristow's own defense of his journalistic venture was: "We have an abiding faith that in the future the west will be reclaimed; that those who have been struggling and battling with hot winds for the last fifteen years will overcome these obstacles, and prosperity will reward their labors in the end, and the great west will produce enough of its products of the soil to sustain an enormous population."[3]

Irrigation was a complex frontier problem, and after 1890, Bristow was drawn into it, as were most of his contemporaries. Transplanted eastern methods of farming could succeed west of the 98th meridian, or roughly the western two-thirds of Kansas, only when rainfall was above average. Once drought hit the frontier, depression followed and the future of agriculture looked dark. Population declined as crops failed in the dry years of the late 1880's. In 1889, 81,279 people were counted in Kansas west of the 100th meridian, but by 1895 only 49,850 souls could be found in the same area.

In 1890 irrigation was not new to Kansas. One of the earliest irrigation projects had been built in 1870 by soldiers at Fort Wallace on the Smoky Hill River to provide water for the fort's lawns and four acres of vegetables. In the 1880's there were many small systems in the Arkansas River Valley, especially around Garden City, Kansas. When the residents of Colorado diverted too much water from the rivers and streams that flowed through Kansas, experiments were started using the vast reservoir of underground water in the river valleys. Windmills with small retaining ponds were brought into use, and a slogan developed for the farm that could not be reached by a river or a brook called for a "windmill and a pond on every farm."

Crop yields were greatly improved through irrigation during the early 1880's. The editor of the Garden City *Irrigator* wrote on July 6, 1882: "The growth of our irrigated crops is so wonderful to behold and simply immense. We could get up a whole state fair of our own, this fall, if our farmers would 'trot out' the best they have."

Irrigation farming, however, was harrassed by many problems during the early experiments. Canal beds were often porous, flumes and diversion dams gave way from flood waters, pumps were costly, and credit was scarce. Enthusiasm for irrigation lessened, therefore, when rainfall increased.

During the dry years from 1887 to 1895, interest was renewed, and by 1893 it had taken on the characteristics of a crusade. Bristow used his editorial power to encourage new irrigation ventures, becoming one of the most energetic spokesmen for the cause. Closely associated with him were three Kansans: Martin Mohler, secretary of the State Board of Agriculture; James S. Emery, who became a national lecturer; and E. R. Moses, president of the Interstate Irrigation Association, founded at Salina in 1893. These energetic advocates were soon known throughout the irrigated areas of the West.

Bristow became active in the irrigation program in 1892, and he was a prime mover in the formation of the Interstate Irrigation Association in late September, 1893. Delegates came from Wyoming, Colorado, Nebraska, Missouri, Oklahoma, Texas, and Kansas to participate in an excellent program headed by national leaders. Moses was elected president and Bristow was made secretary, and an executive committee representing the midwestern states was organized to govern the new association. Bristow was also secretary for the Kansas Irrigation Association, which met at the same time.

After the Salina meeting Bristow continued to work for the cause of irrigation as an organizer and speaker. He took an active part in the International Irrigation Congress in Los Angeles in

October, at which delegates formally supported the creation of a Department of Irrigation in the President's cabinet, the control of public lands by the states, the establishment of permanent irrigation boards at the state level, and the development of a carefully written set of irrigation laws. Bristow attended the state meeting in Wichita in November, 1893, and was instrumental in the selection of Howard V. Hinckley as consulting engineer for the state organization.

As secretary of the interstate association, Bristow planned the program for a meeting at North Platte, Nebraska, in December, 1893. Some four hundred delegates met to study the results of irrigation by the use of artesian wells, windmills, and gasoline engines. The delegates also considered ways to perfect the interstate organization. Major John Powell, director of the United States Geological Survey, Emery, and Bristow were among the chief speakers.[4]

Bristow assisted in the organization of the Omaha Irrigation Convention which met March 21-22, 1894. He was chairman of the resolutions committee and made a forceful speech on the need for an interstate organization. At the Omaha meeting the merits of pump irrigation and the types of machinery that could be used effectively were discussed, and the delegates pressed for congressional appropriations to test the feasibility of irrigation from artesian wells.[5] In Omaha, Bristow met and caught the enthusiasm of such leaders as F. W. Mondell and Francis E. Warren of Wyoming; I. A. Fort and William F. Cody of Nebraska; and Major Powell and his successor, Charles D. Wolcott. He returned to Kansas and visited many new plants run by windmills. He studied the crops that responded best to irrigation practices and assisted in setting up some forty new local societies. At the same time he was collecting and editing material for the *Irrigation Farmer*.

In early September, 1894, he found time to serve as one of the thirty-two delegates from Kansas to the Third National Irrigation Congress, which met in Denver, Colorado. This meeting was attended by delegates from nearly every state in the Union, as well as from Canada and Mexico. At the close of the congress, Bristow and Emery visited the potato fields at Greeley, the experimental plots at Fort Collins, and the peach orchards at Grand Junction. They were deeply impressed by the substantial gain the people of Colorado had made in the production of alfalfa, vegetables, melons, and fruit by irrigation.[6] When Bristow returned, he visited the Finney County Agricultural Society and Fair in October. There were over one hundred pumping plants in the county at that time, and one of the special features of the fair was an exhibit of all types of pumping machinery then in use, particularly windmills.[7]

The 1894 Kansas Irrigation Association meeting was held at Hutchinson, November 23–24. There were papers on the experiments that had been conducted in various counties in 1893 and 1894. Great emphasis was placed on growing alfalfa. Moses reviewed one year of irrigation in the state. Ira C. Hubbell, manager of Fairbanks-Morse Company in Kansas City, read a detailed report on pumping machinery. William E. Smythe, editor of *Irrigation Age,* was on the program. Governor-elect Morrill attended the meeting. Francis H. Newell, who had made surveys of water resources for the United States Department of Agriculture, was present throughout the meetings, and former Governor L. B. Prince of New Mexico gave a light and humorous talk on the irrigation of the "very arid regions." Bristow attended the meeting and reported its proceedings in detail in the December and January issues of the *Irrigation Farmer.*

It was through the columns of the *Irrigation Farmer* that Bristow exercised his greatest influence on the "irrigation revival" of the 1890's. The journal, which began publication in February, 1894, "met a more cordial reception than its promoter had at first expected." In the first four months the circulation reached eleven states. There were demands for it in northern Texas, several readers in Wyoming, South Dakota, and New Mexico, and large sales in Colorado, Nebraska, and Kansas.[8] On March 8, 1894, M. A. Wilson of Atwood, Kansas, wrote Bristow that he got twelve subscriptions in thirty minutes. The subscription rate was one dollar a year, but the journal could be purchased at club rates of fifty cents a member.

During the first year of publication, irrigation was the chief topic considered in the *Irrigation Farmer*. Bristow reprinted some of the best scientific articles written during the time and described the experiences of individual farmers who were conducting experiments. He also selected from midwestern newspapers clippings that showed the gains made by irrigation. Reports were published on how to build reservoirs, the best locations for windmills, the most suitable crops, and the amount of water that could be obtained from various kinds of well equipment.

Bristow constantly spoke out against the false concepts and the sham that often accompany experimental movements. He was hard on the "rainmaker." In the August, 1894, issue of *Irrigation Farmer* he wrote that the drought had not only destroyed the corn and burned up the pasture, but it had "also killed the rainmakers." "We are sorry," Bristow wrote, "to lose corn and have the pastures dry up so badly, but if the rainmaker is effectively squelched the drought has not been without advantage." In December, 1895, Bristow wrote that the rainmaker was "a thing of the past; he was a fraud; an ingenious tramp who played upon the cupidity and superstitions of the people and worked them the same as a sleight-of-hand performer. How ridiculous and silly for a community to pay five hundred or a thousand dollars to a man for assuming to bring rain from cloudless skies."

In February of 1895, Bristow divided the *Irrigation Farmer* into separate sections devoted to horticulture, forestry, fishing, poultry, and general irrigation. On March 2, 1895, a fire destroyed the printing plant, and all that Bristow saved were the subscription books and the ledger. He found himself begging his subscribers for back copies so that he could complete his file.[9]

From the *Irrigation Farmer* one can discover the philosophy of Bristow and his contemporaries. For many western settlers it was "irrigate or migrate." How could the farmer adjust agriculture to the new conditions of climate and rainfall? Bristow, like many others, was seeking to prove that the farmer could survive on 160 acres of land, even in a semi-arid area. He believed that a few acres under irrigation were more valuable than 320 acres left to the wiles and whims of Mother Nature. Seldom did he mention the idea of a farm surplus; he stressed, instead, the ideas of self-sufficiency and the improved conditions which would come to the farmer through the small-scale production of a wide variety of garden and farm crops under an irrigation system. The idea of a self-sufficient farmer would not be accepted today, and, in turn, it seems clear that Bristow would not have supported large scale "dry-farming" in the early 1890's.

For a time Bristow became a champion of forestry and recommended five acres of forest on every 160-acre farm.[10] He also propagandized effectively for both state and federal assistance in making surveys and conducting experiments with pump irrigation. His drive for state assistance was successful in 1895. However, his chief proposal for meeting the farm crisis was the continuation of small holdings equipped with low-cost windmills, pumps, and reservoirs. He urged his readers to seek their economic salvation in this manner and cautioned that state and federal assistance would come too slowly for immediate relief.

In 1894 and 1895, Kansas saw experiments that might be described as a "windmill revival." Many farmers built the Jumbo, or Great Mogul, mill themselves. It was patterned like the stern paddle wheel which had been used to propel the early steamboats. The wheel was mounted on a box-like stand with the lower half of the wheel enclosed. When the wind struck the exposed upper half, the wheel turned to furnish power. Frequently a pump was connected to each end of the wheel shaft. There were many low-cost commercial windmills on the market, several of which were advertised in the *Irrigation Farmer*. Some of the leading ones were the Gem, the Fairbanks-Morse, the Aeromotor, the Halladay, the Double Header Challenge, the Ideal, the Eclipse, the Crane, and the Gause. Other firms, producing cylinders, pumps, casing, well points, ditchers, graders, scrapers, and tile, also advertised in Bristow's journal.

Most irrigators, who depended on windmills or gasoline engines for power, built storage reservoirs to hold the water when they were not irrigating, thereby enabling the mills to run day and night. Reservoir building became a science in itself. Many of the farmers built small reservoirs approximately sixty by one hundred feet with retaining walls from three to four feet high. Occasionally someone built a storage system that covered one or two acres. The retaining walls had to be packed, and the bottoms of the reservoirs had to be compacted to make the soil less porous. Often the earth was covered with water, and horses or cattle were driven across the bottom—through a "loblolly"—until the soil was firmly packed. Some builders used clay on the bottoms of the reservoirs. The windmill and reservoir were located on high ground, and ditches were constructed to carry the water to the crops. Occasionally tile pipe was used to carry the water. In some instances the reservoirs were kept filled the year round and were stocked with fish; this also provided ice that could be stored for summer use. Farmers found that irrigating during the fall and winter produced better crops in the coming year and made farming a few more acres possible. Along the river valleys farmers occasionally dug reservoirs lower than the level of the river bed and allowed them to fill by seepage from the river. The water was then pumped from the reservoir to the irrigated land.

A few farmers built earthen dams across gullies to collect storm water for irrigation. One of the largest storm-water systems was built by George M. Munger on his "Catalpa Farm" eight miles north of Eureka, Kansas. Bristow visited this farm for two days and wrote a detailed description of Munger's work. His land lay between Fall River on the east and the Flint Hills on the west, and on it he had built a dam 2,600 feet long, 40 feet high, and 192 feet wide at the base, forming a 207-acre lake. Steam-powered engines could take 4,000 gallons a day to the highest point of the land; a greater volume could be supplied to the lower land. All together Munger was irrigating 650 acres of land. He had planted 25,000 trees on a 500-acre orchard tract, which produced several varieties of apples, peaches, and pears; and 150 acres were planted with forest trees.[11]

In addition to Munger's large project, there were several small storm-water projects in the state. For the year 1894 the Kansas Board of Irrigation Survey and Experiment reported that 180 farmers used streams, 556 used wells, and 8 used storm waters as their source of supply. By the close of 1895, out of 1,335 farmers who reported on 11,823 acres under irrigation, 253 used streams and 998 used wells. It was estimated that in 1896 there were some 22,000 acres of land in Kansas under irrigation. The chief source of power was windmills, but a few farmers used steam or gasoline engines.[12]

The individual irrigation plants that were built in 1894 and 1895 were sometimes costly and disappointing. Their lack of success was due largely to the lack of scientific information on the availability of underground water and to the general belief that all wells could be developed with equal success. There was also a tendency on the part of some promoters to exaggerate the success of the early projects, especially the number of acres that could be irrigated by one well. The Interstate Irrigation Association and many local associations began to press for state assistance for surveying the water resources and for securing scientific data on the efficiency of pump systems.

Governor Morrill, no doubt greatly influenced by his private secretary, Joseph Bristow, and by his own sincere interest in land usage, recommended that the Kansas legislature establish a special board for study and experimentation. Accordingly, in 1895 the legislature created a Board of Irrigation Survey and Experiment.[13] The bill provided for a board, appointed by the governor, to consist of three active and two advisory members. The work of the board would be limited to an area west of the 98th meridian. The state would construct twenty experimental wells, not over one to each county, on unoccupied school lands or on forty-acre tracts donated by landowners. The school lands in the area would be withdrawn from sale for a period of two years. The salary of the active board members was set at $1,000 a year, and a total of $30,000 was appropriated for the experimental wells. The bill directed the board to map the boundaries and determine the quantity of the underflow water, to measure the amount of water in the streams, and to collect general information on irrigation. Governor Morrill appointed D. M. Frost of Garden City as president of the board, William B. Sutton of Russell as secretary, and M. B. Tomblin of Goodland as the third active member of the board. George T. Fairchild, president of the Kansas State Agricultural College, and Professor Erasmus Haworth of the Department of Geology at the University of Kansas were selected as advisers to the board. These men were deeply interested in the problems of irrigation, and all were close friends of Bristow's.[14]

The board started immediately to put the program into operation. It used the services of the personnel at Kansas State Agricultural College, the University of Kansas, and the United States Geological Survey whenever possible. Wells were sunk on unoccupied school lands and on ten tracts donated by individuals,[15] and the first state pumping station was put into use in early July, 1895, at Goodland, Kansas. Tests were made, records of costs and production were kept, and the efficiency of pumps and windmills was studied. All of the information was reported to the legislature in 1897. The board had spent its funds wisely and efficiently. At the close of the survey the state held irrigation property valued at $18,000.

The board made several recommendations to the next legislature. It urged the creation of a permanent office with a clerk. It recommended that the private land be returned to the original owners; that experiments should not be confined to school lands; that some of the projects should be turned over to the experiment stations where federal funds were available; and that the Fish Commission should be allotted three or four of the projects for experimental hatcheries. It also pointed out that there must be further mapping of the underground water supply.[16]

In the election of 1896 the Populists swept the state ticket. In striving for economy the newly elected governor recommended no appropriations for the work of the Board of Irrigation Survey and Experiment. The legislature created a new Department of Forestry and Irrigation and instructed the commissioner to sell the property of the old board. The land donated by individuals to the state for pumping stations was returned.[17]

This action was not entirely governed by political expediency. More plentiful rainfall in 1896 increased the yields of corn and winter wheat. Late in 1896 a gradual advance in prices (which continued in 1897) helped to eliminate much of the agitation for state aid to irrigation. In 1897 the corn crop fell by some seventy million bushels, but cattle and wheat production increased, and advancing prices continued the prosperity of the state. The new commissioner of Forestry and Irrigation, E. D. Wheeler, summed up the situation in his first report when he wrote, "The wealth and comfort irrigation has brought to the people of the state are well worth all it cost and yet we have made only a beginning." Wheeler emphasized the success Kansans had had with orchards and gardens under irrigation and wrote that there was not a county in central and western Kansas where irrigation was not practiced. He estimated that one-half a family's living was produced in gardens.[18]

Bristow published the last edition of the *Irrigation Farmer* in November, 1896. The lessening interest in irrigation and the decrease in income from advertising perhaps helped him decide to discontinue the paper. Moreover, he was determined to seek an appointive position from the newly elected McKinley administration, and he hoped to move to Washington the following spring.

As a participant for two and one-half years in the "crusade" for irrigation, Bristow had learned many valuable lessons. He had become well acquainted with the economic and social problems of the people and was now advocating state and federal aid for the solution of these problems. His name was well known in the state and to national leaders in the fields of reclamation and irrigation. A decade later, when he entered the United States Senate, he was conversant with these issues and continued his campaign for federal assistance in the irrigation of the Great Plains. Under both McKinley and Theodore Roosevelt, Bristow was able to observe and counsel effectively on matters pertaining to the Midwest. From 1897 to 1905, in Washington, he came ever closer to the realities of American political life.

3

Postal Years

In 1896 politicians throughout the United States wondered how the voters in Kansas, the most strongly Populist state in the nation, would perform. The traditional patterns of voting in Kansas had been upset since 1890, and the mood of the voters was unpredictable. The political distress over Cleveland's stand on gold, his failure with the income tax and tariff, and the slowly receding economic depression made the outcome of the November election difficult to forecast.

The People's party had proposed many remedies for the existing political and economic problems, but a tendency was developing on the part of the leaders to stress one single remedy: the free and unlimited coinage of silver. After the Republican victory in 1894, there was talk of a fusion between the Democratic and Populist leaders, and when William Jennings Bryan became a candidate for the Presidency and seized upon the issue of free silver, both Democratic and Populist leaders in Kansas readily endorsed his candidacy. Bryan, feeling that the state was safe for "Popocracy," did not visit Kansas.[1]

In 1895 there had been genuine opposition among the Republicans at Topeka to McKinley's candidacy. Some Republicans favored free silver as a modest proposal for inflation. Even the conservative Charles E. Curtis was an advocate of free silver for a time. Cyrus Leland and Joseph Bristow opposed the stand of the Topeka "gang" and remained firm for sound money. They brought Jonathan Dolliver from Iowa to speak before the Republican League in 1895. Dolliver urged the Kansas Republicans to follow Iowans who had discarded the silver heresy earlier. Other elements of friction came from Republicans who felt that Governor Morrill was not working hard enough and that a younger leader should be found.[2] Nevertheless, harmony seemed to prevail at the Republican state convention in 1896. William McKinley was endorsed and Governor Morrill was renominated by acclamation. Discontented political elements within the state sought refuge in local tickets for the Populist party, the national Democratic party, the National party, and the ever-present Prohibition party, which appeared under four different political banners.

Some of the most effective campaigners in the Republican party were sent to Kansas to keep the 1894 victory intact. Early in July, Bristow invited Senator J. M. Thurston of Nebraska and "Colonel" John M. Mason, a senatorial candidate from Illinois, to speak at the state convention. Later Thomas B. Reed, Garret A. Hobart, "Corporal" James Tanner, and Edward S. Taylor toured the state. H. C. Goodman of Chicago spoke to the German settlements, and President Carl A. Swensson of Bethany College spoke to the Swedes in Kansas. Among the many state leaders were Senators Baker and Long, William A. Calderhead, Joseph R. Burton, Snyder S. Kirkpatrick, John J. Ingalls, Thomas A. McNeal, and Edward W. Hoch.[3]

The Democratic-Populist fusion, however, swept the state with hurricane fury. Bryan and Sewall polled 171,180 votes, Bryan and Watson 46,194, and McKinley and Hobart 159,541. Not only did the state's electoral votes go to Bryan, but the Democrats also won all the state offices, six congressional seats, and a majority in both houses of the Kansas legislature. Case Broderick and Charles Curtis were the only two successful Republican candidates for the

House of Representatives. Leedy defeated Morrill by a vote of 168,041 to 160,330. With twenty-eight Democrats or Populists in the state senate and seventy-five in the lower house, Kansas could soon place two Democrats in the United States Senate. Bristow, who had worked hard to keep the party lines intact during the campaign, described the Republican defeat in the Ottawa *Herald*: "We are defeated in Kansas, but there is one consoling thought; it took the combined forces of populism, crankism, the new democracy, mossbackism, fiatism, socialism and chronic dyspepsia to defeat us, and then the defeat was only about 5,000 plurality."[4]

The election of 1896 not only brought a signal defeat to the Republican party in Kansas, but it also greatly weakened the structure of the People's party. Although many of the People's party reformers never lost their impact on the state, the eventual death of the party was only a decade away. In the election of 1898 the Populists secured only 4 per cent of the nationwide vote, and Kansas contributed one-fourth of this weak 4 per cent.[5]

While Bristow's party was defeated in Kansas, it won the national election in 1896 and elected a President. As secretary to the Republican state central committee, Bristow had kept his political contacts with national leaders in the party, and now he began casting about for an appointive position from President-elect McKinley, whose candidacy he had supported since early 1894. McKinley had made a deep and lasting impression on the young party secretary during his short political tour in Kansas in October of that year. At that time Bristow had observed that McKinley's voice was "neither musical nor especially strong," but it was "sympathetic and very effective." When the local committee stopped the train some distance from the station in Hutchinson to avoid the crowd, McKinley had remonstrated and said "a man in public life cannot afford to avoid the people." This, too, had impressed Bristow. In later years, in describing the tour, Bristow wrote that he was delighted with McKinley's personality: "His personality was charming. I liked him. I wanted to see him President."[6] Even after a four-year stint in McKinley's official family, Bristow retained a deep respect for, and lasting confidence in, William McKinley.

During the campaign of 1896, McKinley had asked his secretary, Joseph P. Smith, an Ohio newspaper man and a most loyal friend, to look after the campaign in Kansas. Bristow became well acquainted with Smith during the campaign, and Smith invited him to stop at Canton, Ohio, on his way to the inaugural ceremonies. Publicly, Bristow was going to Washington for pleasure, but privately he was determined to look for a federal appointment. He had first thought of the consul generalship at Havana, but that position was not vacant. Cyrus Leland had suggested Bristow as a possible private secretary for McKinley, but Bristow did not feel that he wanted such a place. Smith now suggested that Bristow consider the position of fourth assistant postmaster-general.[7] The Kansas delegation in Washington supported Smith's suggestion and urged Bristow to accept the position if McKinley approved.

Bristow had a short visit with McKinley at Canton. Early in the negotiations Mark Hanna opposed the appointment on the grounds of Bristow's youth and inexperience. Hanna wanted a man more closely connected with the Republican National Committee. There was also a concerted effort by Republicans in the Kansas legislature, some of whom by this time had differences with the state party secretary, to defeat Bristow. Some of the Republicans were backing Giles H. Lamb, a state senator from Woodson County. Republicans in the Kansas senate signed telegrams protesting the rumored appointment, which were sent to the postmaster-general, James A. Gary, in care of the Kansas delegation in Washington.[8] On March 18, Cyrus Leland and the Kansas delegation tabled the protest. On the same day five Republican state senators who had supposedly signed one of the first telegrams wired the postmaster-general to remove their names from the protest. Senator Isaac Lambert declared his name had been placed on the original telegram fraudulently.[9] With the opposition greatly weakened at Topeka, the Kansans in Washington pressed harder for Bristow. Hanna withdrew his opposition and McKinley made the appointment. Hanna declared that Bristow was probably the youngest man to hold the position and in his brusque way greeted Bristow with the declaration that "this is the most important office, politically, in the gift of the administration." Bristow, according to Hanna, could have the office, "but no other Kansas man could."[10]

Many of Bristow's fellow Republican editors praised McKinley for his excellent selection. The Topeka representative of the Kansas City *Star* was accurate in his appraisal of Bristow: McKinley, according to the *Star's* reporter, "could have made a more popular selection . . . but his [Bristow's] worst enemies concede his peculiar fitness for the place." As a campaigner Bristow had been "resourceful and alert," and "many of the flanking movements on the enemy" credited to Leland were of Bristow's "conception and execution." The reporter declared that Bristow came from sturdy stock and was "never given to drink or the tobacco habit." He was a man who had the patience for details. He had made enemies because he was "blunt and straight forward and to the point." He was not an adroit man, but sincere; "a good hater" who had "no patience with shams." He was a man, continued the reporter, who liked "to fight in the open" and wanted "his forces and allies to be inspired by pure patriotism." He was also a willful man. If he saw his way clearly, he had no patience with men who took a different view or who had another method. In the eyes of the reporter, it was this last trait that had made Bristow "obnoxious" to many men in his own party.[11]

It must be conceded that granting the fourth assistant postmaster-generalship to a candidate from a state in which the party had been defeated was surprising. In a sense, McKinley's action expressed a hope that the continued cultivation of the political soil in Kansas might develop a stronger Republican plant in the years to come. Political life in Washington was to be greatly influenced by the award; Bristow proved to be an efficient administrator. His courageous handling of the Cuban postal scandals in 1900, under President McKinley, made him "man of the hour," and his workmanship three years later in investigating the postal scandals under President Theodore Roosevelt made him "man of the year."

It was an established practice by 1897 that the directors of the Post Office Department were selected because of their skill in political management and their closeness to the inner party circle. McKinley's selection of Bristow as fourth assistant postmaster-general was no exception to the rule. Bristow served under two Presidents and four postmaster-generals before he resigned from the office in 1905.

In selecting his cabinet McKinley had offered the postmaster-generalship to Mark Hanna. Hanna declined and sought a seat in the United States Senate. He recommended Henry C. Payne of Milwaukee to the President for postmaster-general. Payne, vice-chairman of the Republican National Committee in 1896 and a leading political strategist, had directed much of the publicity for the Republicans during the recent campaign. McKinley did not like Payne and, to the surprise of the party leaders, chose James A. Gary of Baltimore for postmaster-general. Gary had been active in party politics and assisted in delivering the electoral vote of his state to McKinley, the first Republican victory in Maryland in the presidential contests since the Civil War. Gary was a skillful businessman, but he was not, in any sense, the patronage dispenser for McKinley. Much of this task fell to Hanna and Perry S. Heath, then first assistant postmaster-general. Heath was a news-paperman from Ohio, who had been closely associated with McKinley in politics. There is ample evidence in the McKinley Papers to show the work of these two men in the disposal of the patronage. Gary remained in the cabinet for a little over one year; he resigned partly because of his health and also because he did not favor the entry of the United States into the war with Spain.[12] McKinley appointed Charles E. Smith, editor of the Philadelphia *Press,* as Gary's successor. Smith had written much of the platform for the Republican party in 1896 and after McKinley's election had served as a press agent for the administration. He lost the support of the reformers when he defended McKinley's removal of certain positions from the classified civil service. Smith served until 1902.[13] President Roosevelt then selected Henry Payne, Hanna's original suggestion to McKinley. This appointment drew protests from the reformers who were anxious to lessen the spoils system in the postal service. Payne had directed the details of the campaign in 1896 for Hanna, a well-known foe of the merit system. Later, Payne was vice-chairman of the Republican National Committee. Roosevelt defended his selection of Payne on the grounds that he needed a capable political adviser as postmaster-general. After Payne's death in October, 1904, Roosevelt promoted the first assistant postmaster-general, Robert J. Wynne, to postmaster-general.[14]

At the time of Bristow's appointment, President McKinley instructed Gary and Bristow that presidential postmasters were to serve out their commissions, unless there was cause for their removal, and that fourth-class postmasters were to serve a four-year term. He insisted that there should not be reckless nor precipitate removals and added that he did not want Bristow to be known as a headsman or spoilsman. Gary followed McKinley's orders, much to the displeasure of the Republican leaders. In his year of service he removed only 129 presidential postmasters and only 70 resigned. Bristow believed that McKinley was sincere and in spite of terrific political pressure tried to hold the line.[15] A friend of the Bristow family told the story of Joe's attendance at a formal affair in a business suit when all the other guests were in formal dress. Bristow did not have a dress suit at the time. President McKinley noticed his embarrassment and invited Bristow to sit by him throughout the evening. Bristow never forgot the President's kind act. This was the McKinley that Joe knew and he was determined to conduct his office in the manner that would not embarrass his chief.[16]

When Bristow entered office, the Post Office Department was the last stronghold of the spoilsmen. President Grover Cleveland had placed many federal employees under the merit system. Clerks in the Post Office Department were on the classified list, but postmasters throughout the nation were still subject to political patronage. One of the many duties of the fourth assistant postmaster-general was the supervision of the fourth-class post offices.

Bristow had charge of 69,754 such offices during his first year in Washington.

There were three main divisions under Bristow's supervision in 1897: the division of appointments, the division of bonds and commissions, and the division of post office inspectors. In the division of appointments all papers relating to an appointment were briefed, jacketed, and filed for the consideration of the fourth assistant, the postmaster-general, and the President. Although the fourth-class postmasters were appointed by the President, it was the division chief who was responsible for all the paper work. The appointment division was under political pressure at all times. Postmaster-General Gary received approximately ninety-five thousand letters regarding appointments in the three weeks ending March 29, 1897. In the two months previous to McKinley's inauguration, the Civil Service Commission was flooded with some eighteen thousand applications for employment. Bristow declared that, within twenty minutes after he took the oath of office, his room was filled with senators, congressmen, and applicants inquiring about the policy which would be followed by the directors of the Post Office Department.[17] In almost every instance the department was governed in the choice of postmasters by the advice and recommendations of the representatives. Rarely did a senator offer advice, unless the position was in his home town or in a large city. It was not difficult to resolve the conflicts in districts represented by Republican congressmen. For the districts where Democrats had been elected a list of referees or advisers was established. Usually a defeated Republican congressman and members of the state committee served as advisers. In the South it was hard to find enough Republicans to fill the vacancies in the post offices. Some referees supported Democrats, and at times Republican postmasters moved about like the carpetbaggers after the Civil War.[18]

To some men this kind of political pressure and supervision would have been distasteful, but Bristow felt that, in some ways, his office was one of the most desirable in Washington. During his early months of service, he met most of the congressmen; he became acquainted with many varied interests of the country and different characteristics of the people. Experience soon seasoned him and he could respond like an "old Washington hand." He found many interests among the congressmen. Some found patronage incidental and frequently distasteful. Others used patronage to strengthen the party or themselves. And there were always the patronage chasers. Bristow told of the comment by the Washington *Post* that if an office were hung on the corner of the moon, Congressman Sydney E. Mudd would get it; the Congressman regarded the *Post's* description as a compliment. From these many congressional contacts Bristow met men who became his friends and supporters.[19] In later years some of these men made up the heart of the progressive movement.

When the policy of allowing the fourth-class postmasters to serve for four years was announced by the division of appointments, the number of complaints against incumbent postmasters increased. Some of the complaints were frivolous; any excuse would serve to get rid of a Democrat. One postmaster, according to a complaint, had an unsightly nose, and one had an offensive breath caused by catarrh. In the South one might be accused of being a former Confederate or of having spoken in a derogatory manner of Negroes. When Bristow received complaints he tried to get the facts. If the incumbent was found to be inefficient, delinquent in his financial accounts, or immoral, he was removed with dispatch.

Cases of removal during the first two years brought little opposition, if Bristow got rid of a Democrat. In later years, if a Republican got into trouble, he was apt to be defended by his congressional supporters regardless of the nature of the crime. Congressmen were known to defend postmasters who had been short in their financial accounts for long periods of time, and some congressmen would refuse to look for a successor to the delinquent incumbent. In these cases Bristow was ably assisted by his chief in the division of appointments, W. R. Spillman of Manhattan, Kansas; but there were times when President McKinley's aid was obtained to override the desires of a congressman.[20]

During the fiscal year ending June 30, 1898, the division of appointments processed the papers for the appointment of 23,496 fourth-class postmasters. These appointments were made to fill vacancies created by 8,200 resignations, 881 deaths, 8,400 expired terms, 2,369 removals, and 3,601 newly established post offices.[21] It was not unusual to create from 1,500 to over 3,000 new offices in a year, but the number declined when the rural free delivery system was established in 1896. During Theodore Roosevelt's first term the R.F.D. was placed under Bristow's supervision, adding a tremendous load to the division. Often 3,000 to 5,000 requests for new routes were presented in one year. The R.F.D. grew rapidly. In 1897 there were 83 routes, and by 1904, Bristow was supervising 24,566 routes. Over 8,000 additional routes were opened in 1905.[22]

The second division under Bristow, the division of bonds and commissions, was always overloaded at the beginning of a new administration. In 1897 the division carried bonds amounting to $68,000,000 and maintained files for the oaths of all assistants and clerks in the postal service. By 1902 the efficiency of the department had reached a high level.

The division of post office inspectors was subdivided into the departments of post office inspectors and mail depredations. Bristow found a great lag in the inspection service when he entered office. There were presidential post offices which had not been inspected for ten years, and a large number of carry-over complaints needed examination. Over one hundred thousand complaints were examined in one year. There is no doubt that Bristow made his greatest contribution in the inspection service. He trained a corps of young men in whom he could put his trust; among them were J. R. (Jack) Harrison of Manhattan, Kansas, W. E. Cochran of Topeka, Kansas, and Carter B. Keene of Maine. Each won an outstanding reputation for his work. Bristow introduced a new bookkeeping system for the inspection service in 1898 and secured greater financial support from Congress for this branch of the service. By 1900 the inspectors were visiting every money-order post office once a year,[23] and the division was receiving enormous newspaper publicity. By 1902 it was most effective and was highly respected.

As fourth assistant postmaster-general, Bristow mastered the internal details of the postal service, initiated reforms, and developed an all-encompassing responsibility for his department. Each year the work load seemed to increase. The growth of cities and the accompanying use of the postal facilities for business purposes added extra pressure to the service, as did the system of free delivery in both urban and rural areas.

Civil service reformers were critical of the handling of personnel in the Post Office Department. They protested the rapid turnover of fourth-class postmasters that resulted from the fact that these positions were not under the classified service. The leaders in the National Civil Service Reform League condemned two types of abuses within the classified service: the practice of "blanketing in" Republican appointees just before a position or an office was classified, and the use of laborers, who were outside the merit system, in classified clerical positions. The Civil Service Commission found that neither Smith nor Gary, as postmaster-general, was cooperative in checking the second abuse.[24] There were few cases of "blanketing in" employees under McKinley because he made few additions to the classified service.

Another worry of the reformers during McKinley's administration was that the President was badgered constantly by Republicans to declassify a number of positions placed under the merit system by President Grover Cleveland. McKinley resisted the grumblings of Hanna and other senators until the preliminary campaign maneuvers in the summer of 1899, but on May 29, 1899, the expected order to declassify was given. This was followed by two or three additional executive orders, and over 9,000 positions were exempted from the merit system.[25] The postal service had some 450 of the exempted positions. The reformers heaped their criticism on the President and further blackened the administration's record by pointing out numerous cases of political activity on the part of Republican postmasters.[26]

For several years the reform press and individuals closely

associated with the politically dominated Post Office Department had hinted that there was corruption within certain postal bureaus. Mark Hanna's ruthless control of the patronage had not improved the situation. If Postmaster-General Smith knew of the laxities, he never moved to correct them. Intense interest was created in the press and in Congress in the spring of 1900 by apparent scandals in the Department of Posts in Cuba. This department was not under the military government, but was directed by the Post Office Department in Washington. Estes G. Rathbone had been appointed director-general of the Department of Posts for Cuba in December, 1898. Rathbone had served as a pension examiner, as the chief of the postal inspectors, and as fourth assistant postmaster-general under previous Republican administrations. He was a close friend of Perry S. Heath, the first assistant postmaster under McKinley. Postmaster-General Smith had given Rathbone full powers to manage the postal affairs in Cuba. Governor General Leonard Wood saw that in this new position Rathbone was living most extravagantly, far beyond the possibilities of his government salary. Upon inquiry Wood found that Rathbone had no private means of support, and he immediately asked the inspector general of the United States Army to investigate the Bureau of Finance in the Cuban postal service. C. F. Neely, the director of the bureau, sailed for the United States the day after the investigation began. Through the Secretary of War, Postmaster-General Smith was asked to arrest Neely, who, evidently on his way to Canada, was arrested by the chief of police in Rochester, New York, and returned to Cuba. Governor General Wood's investigation showed large shortages in the postal accounts and an apparent record of embezzlement that had been going on for several months.[27]

The report of the embezzlements shocked President McKinley. He may have overlooked abuses in the patronage, but he was in no mood to sanction outright fraud and graft in the public service. He backed Governor General Wood in pressing the charges against the grafters and ordered an investigation from Washington. On May 14, 1900, he called Bristow to the White

House and asked him to direct the Cuban investigation. McKinley explained that he had been deeply pained by the Cuban reports, especially because government appointees had been guilty of defrauding United States wards. He felt that the United States had a serious obligation to try to teach the Cubans how to run a government, and he directed Bristow to "be cautious but firm, and to shield no man who had been guilty of wrong doing." Bristow replied that he was willing to go, but pointed out that since the men involved in the Cuban scandals had been recommended by powerful forces in Washington, he would no doubt be subjected to severe criticism. McKinley responded, "As to complaints, leave them to me, I will take care of them." In a few days Bristow, with seven of his most trusted inspectors, left for Cuba, feeling that he had the full support of President McKinley behind him.[28]

On May 19, Rathbone was excluded from his office, and Bristow became the temporary director of Cuban postal affairs. Bristow's investigation, courageous and methodical, was also swift. His chief task was to furnish evidence from which indictments could be secured. Postmaster-General Smith released Bristow's report on July 26, 1900. The greatest graft was through the excessive credit Neely had obtained by the destruction of supercharged stamps. There were instances in which Rathbone had used public funds for private expenses. Neely also had interests in a printing concern in the United States and had run up excessive bills for printing and furniture in the Cuban treasury. W. H. Reeves, an auditor in the War Department, had received $4,600 for conspiring with Neely. Bristow estimated that $131,713.89 had been stolen. Rathbone filed an answer to Bristow's charges through the chairman of a Senate investigating committee in Cuba,[29] but he did not escape trial. He was sentenced to ten years' imprisonment and fined $56,000. Neely and Reeves received similar sentences and each was fined $36,000.[30] Several employees were dismissed or demoted. The entire Cuban postal service was reorganized, and new methods of auditing were established. Bristow's friend Jack Harrison, who spent over twelve months in the reorganization of the Havana postal service, reported that the office had been honeycombed with fraud.[31]

The dispatch with which McKinley had acted brought credit to the administration. Postmaster-General Smith praised Bristow's work, and he wrote in his annual report that Bristow had discharged the "duty confided to him with commendable energy and capacity and unswerving rectitude and vigor." It was estimated that over $100,000 a year would be saved by the reorganization of the general postal service.[32] Bristow was justly proud of his work, but Mark Hanna had a different opinion of it. He tried hard to get the sentences set aside and urged a congressional investigation of Governor General Wood. He furnished funds for Rathbone's bond and was probably the chief figure in securing amnesty for both Neely and Rathbone from the Cuban government. He agreed with Rathbone that Bristow was trying to implicate Perry Heath. Heath was allowed to resign from his position as first assistant postmaster-general, and he returned to Chicago to his old press job at Republican campaign headquarters, soon becoming secretary to the Republican National Committee.

Hanna continued to work against Bristow, indirectly, through Charles Dawes, Comptroller of the Currency and member of the executive committee of the Republican National Committee. He wrote to Dawes that Bristow had fired an official who came from Maryland, a doubtful state in the coming election, and complained that "it seems as if he [Bristow] has no political sense or else is vicious—I think the latter as I have no use for him."[33] Hanna failed to see that the prompt removal and punishment of the grafters in Cuba had created a strong public opinion in favor of McKinley's re-election. Also, it was Bristow, not Hanna, who was growing in public favor. Bristow's thorough work in Cuba had kept him from attending both the state and national Republican conventions, but in spite of this there was a light press flurry suggesting that his name be placed on the McKinley ticket as vice-presidential candidate.[34] In the end, this honor was given to Theodore Roosevelt. Despite strong political opposition from the Hanna forces, Bristow remained as fourth assistant postmaster-general, campaigning in the fall for McKinley. When McKinley died, Bristow's foes again moved in; but his reputation as an honest, courageous, and efficient public servant was not overlooked by President Theodore Roosevelt.

Early in his administration President Roosevelt appointed Henry Payne as postmaster-general. He had been the key man in securing Roosevelt's nomination to the Vice-Presidency and was very active in Republican circles. The reformers split over this appointment. Some felt that the President could not reconcile this selection with his professed friendship for the merit system.[35] But Payne was firm on the tenure policy in the Post Office Department. There were to be no removals until written charges had been sustained. The fourth-class postmasters under Bristow's supervision were given an indefinite term with no removals except on proven charges. Payne hoped to educate congressmen to this informal policy.[36] During his three years in office the rate of removals for presidential and fourth-class postmasters hit a record low, although the 34,334 resignations of fourth-class postmasters was an all-time high. Normally, Roosevelt and Payne followed the recommendations of congressmen in filling vacancies in the postal service, but Roosevelt was skillful in his use of the patronage when he sought congressional support for his favorite legislative proposals; he did not hesitate to discipline congressmen by the denial of patronage. Both Payne and Roosevelt took a moderate stand on the political activity of postmasters, and some gains were made for the merit system. On November 27, 1901, the rural free delivery service was classified, and in 1904 postal clerks were selected by competitive examinations. In 1903 the President and the Civil Service Commission completely reviewed and expanded the civil service rules, giving rise to a conflict of interpretation in Roosevelt's official family on the status of fourth-class postmasters. Eventually the President called upon Charles J. Bonaparte, a political independent and a strong supporter of civil service reform, for a ruling. Bonaparte ruled that fourth-class postmasters were still on the excepted list, a decision that left these positions subject to patronage abuses while Bristow was in office. Bonaparte gave an accurate evaluation of Roosevelt's first term, from the point of view of the civil service reformers, in a letter to Lucius B. Swift, October 31, 1904:

> Like all other human beings, he [Roosevelt] has been guilty of sins both of omission and commission and he has also made mistakes, but take him for all in all, we shall not, I fear, soon see the like of him again as a Civil Service Reformer in the Presidential chair, and certainly not if Parker is elected. Cleveland is the only President whose record can be for a moment compared with his, and I infer from your communication that you think, as I do, that a comparison with Cleveland is decidedly to Roosevelt's advantage.[37]

Bonaparte might well have added that Roosevelt's prompt and effective prosecution of new scandals in the Post Office Department on the eve of the 1904 election had raised the President in the esteem of the civil service reformers.

The exposure of the Cuban scandals gave impetus to the old rumors that widespread scandals existed in the postal affairs in Washington and in many of the other large city post offices. These purported wrongdoings ranged from the violation of the civil service rules to large-scale graft and bribery in the purchasing of postal machines and supplies. Prominent businessmen, as well as government employees, were under suspicion. Late in 1902, Postmaster-General Payne discussed with President Roosevelt the need for an investigation and secured an increase of $6,000 in appropriations from Congressman E. F. Loud, chairman of the Committee on Post Offices and Post Roads, for the investigation. The investigation was scheduled to begin as soon as Congress adjourned.[38] Loud did not publicize the reasons for the increase in appropriations, and the press first reported the irregularities in early March, 1903, when George W. Beavers, head of the division of salaries and allowances, resigned on charges of bribery and graft. Both Payne and Roosevelt were absent from Washington at the time, and the press was full of rumors of the needed investigation.

On March 7, 1903, Bristow was directed by Payne to undertake the investigation. Bristow's work in Cuba was now to be of great value to him. Payne returned to Washington and immediately met the press on April 13. His department was demoralized, with charges and countercharges flying in all directions. Payne explained the secret appropriation and announced that Bristow would be in charge of the investigation, unlimited by anyone. This was affrmed by President Roosevelt on April 27 in a public letter to Payne, announcing his support of Bristow's investigation.[39]

Bristow now faced a huge and politically dangerous task. He had won the hatred of Mark Hanna in the past, and many of Hanna's friends were bound to use political pressure against the chief investigator. Men high in the Republican party's councils were under suspicion. The mugwumps and the Democrats could, as William Allen White wrote, "beat out Roosevelt's brains" with the scandals and defeat his bid for the Presidency in 1904.[40] Friction over the scandals might also destroy the President's legislative program. Bristow's chief task was to conduct an impartial inquiry for facts which could be used by federal attorneys to secure bills of indictment. If he erred, congressmen would press Roosevelt, as they had McKinley, to end his service in the Post Office Department. Once again he turned to the best men in the postal inspection service. Over fifty inspectors were on the job, and at times the services of secret service men were utilized.

Tracing the political and financial activities of employees who had split commissions, accepted bribes, and conspired to defraud the government in purchasing contracts was difficult from the beginning. Bank accounts, canceled checks, travel funds, bills of lading, and all kinds of personal records were carefully scrutinized in the search for evidence that would lead to indictment. Prominent officeholders were removed or given leaves of absence in order to give the investigators free access to the records. James N. Tyner, assistant attorney general for the Post Office Department, was dismissed. He was a prominent figure in the Republican party; he had been first assistant postmaster-general and for a short time head of the department.[41] In May, Bristow asked Payne to grant a leave to August W. Machen, superintendent of the free delivery service. Machen was replaced by M. C. Fosner, a postal inspector, and Payne transferred the entire R.F.D. to Bristow's already overloaded division.[42] Machen was later proved to be one of the greatest grafters in the service. He was accused of forging warrants, selling mining stock in a company which he owned to postal employees, and accepting bribes from the owners of a patent device he had purchased for the department. He was indicted on the last charge.

Payne, who wanted to conduct the investigation quietly and secretly, was denounced as being evasive and shrinking. He frequently tried to play down the importance of the scandals, but "trial by press" was in the saddle, especially when the scandals smelled much like the Whiskey Ring scandals under President Grant. In May new charges appeared. Seymour W. Tulloch, a former cashier in the Washington post office, charged that many employees of the local office had been put in their positions for political reasons by former Postmaster-General Smith and former First Assistant Postmaster-General Perry Heath, now secretary of the Republican National Committee. Tulloch declared he had been removed from office because he had objected to the elevation of laborers to classified positions without competitive examinations and to financial irregularities in the local office. Payne labeled Tulloch's charges "hot air." Henry Cabot Lodge, who constantly dreaded the political implications of the scandals, wrote to Roosevelt on May 20, 1903, that he was very disturbed by what Payne was saying.[43] Lodge felt that Payne was either greatly deceived or that he failed to appreciate the gravity of the situation. Roosevelt cautioned Payne on his public utterances, and Bristow assigned three inspectors to trace Heath's record.[44]

Payne and Roosevelt were deeply disturbed by the increasing number of accusations. The work of investigation was slow and this added to their uneasiness. On May 21, Lodge assured Roosevelt that he was certain "we can depend on Bristow." A few days later he wrote that "Bristow, of whom my opinion rises constantly, greatly to my surprise, has already succeeded in making a case on Machen of a penitentiary offense, and that, in my opinion, is only a small part of it."[45] By mid-July, Payne wrote Roosevelt that he could "see the end" of the investigation, praising Bristow's work. On August 20, Bristow reported to Payne that there was evidence that one contractor had paid Machen over $10,000. Bristow assured Payne that the corruption was within the Post Office Department, that it was promoted by officers in the department, but that it had not reached the general postal service. He felt that Payne might grow impatient at the delay in closing out the investigation but there was no way "of hastening any faster."[46]

There is ample evidence in the official postal correspondence in the National Archives to show that Payne was highly cooperative with his chief investigator, in spite of the delays. Hardly a week passed that Payne did not send new leads to Bristow, urging speedy investigation of the accusations. Late in 1903 and early in 1904 there were numerous investigations in the offices outside Washington. Most of these resulted in a request for the offender's resignation. Each case emphasized clearly the need for constant vigilance in a public service which employed thousands of persons.[47]

When the investigation was first made public, some of Roosevelt's close friends urged him to secure the services of politically independent lawyers to assist the Attorney General with the prosecutions. Lodge went so far as to advise keeping Republicans off the special counsel, and Roosevelt chose Holmes Conrad and Charles J. Bonaparte for the task.[48] Conrad was a lifelong Democrat who had served the federal government under both Cleveland and McKinley, and Bonaparte was a political independent.[49] On June 27, 1903, Bonaparte wrote to his brother, Jerome, that he had been invited by the President to assist in the prosecution of any persons connected with the scandals. He complained that the appointment would interfere with his summer plans, but he presumed that he would receive a "reasonable compensation" as the government was still solvent.[50] When the time came for compensation, he wrote Conrad that he was going to charge "what he would a wealthy client."[51]

Conrad and Bonaparte were given only two assignments at first; one was to investigate the Tulloch charges. The two men became deeply involved in their work, and both conferred frequently with Bristow about the various charges. Since neither had had experience in presenting indictments to a grand jury, an assistant United States attorney at Chicago was ordered to Washington to assist in writing the charges.[52] At first Conrad and Bonaparte were to assist only in such cases as the Attorney General designated, but late in July, Bonaparte visited President Roosevelt and found that the President was impatient with the "meager results" which had been attained. Roosevelt broadened the assignment so that Conrad and Bonaparte were to review all the work of the postal inspectors. Bonaparte wrote, on August 1, that the investigation "has been and is still" an immense task, "and so far as I can yet judge," one carried on *"most zealously"* by those who had been entrusted with it.[53] In a later letter Bonaparte described the situation in Washington as "interesting to a civil service reformer" since the abuses and scandals in the Post Office Department were "evidently and unmistakably" due to "spoils" politicians and substantially "to nothing else." Bonaparte felt that other departments were undoubtedly guilty, but stated emphatically that ever since Perry Heath had become first assistant postmaster-general, graft sprouted in the Post Office Department like "weeds in a neglected field."[54]

From the time of his appointment as chief investigator, Bristow and his crew of inspectors worked as they had never worked before. On June 13 the Civil Service Commission issued the first official report, which bore out many of the Tulloch charges. Immediately former Postmaster-General Smith publicly answered the Civil Service Commission accusations. Smith insisted that extra employees had been put in the Washington office, not for political reasons, but to care for the increased demands brought on by the Spanish-American War. He admitted that many laborers had been transferred to clerical positions without the use of competitive examinations, but he insisted that he had made only one personal political appointment. He accused Commissioner John R. Procter of going out of his way "needlessly and wantonly as I think" to attack the department while Smith was head of it.[55] Bristow made a preliminary report in June, and his final report was completed in October; by July, however, the results of his investigation were becoming apparent. Four high-ranking officials were removed: George W. Beavers, head of salaries and allowances; James N. Tyner, assistant attorney general; August W. Machen, superintendent of free delivery service; and James T. Metcalf, superintendent of the postal money-order division. Thirteen subordinates either resigned or were removed. Bristow's final report reached Conrad and Bonaparte in November. The original report contained 373 typewritten pages. It listed thirty-one persons who had been indicted with a total of seventy-six indictments. Conrad and Bonaparte condensed Bristow's report to fifty-one pages.[56]

The report was filled with detailed accounts of the offenses that had been examined. The charges included the improper disposition of public funds, the appointment of clerks without proper examination, the employment of persons who had rendered no service to the government, increased rentals for properties held by congressmen or their constituents, unwarranted salary raises for postmasters and clerks because of congressional pressure, demotion of employees who had honestly tried to fulfill their duties, the failure to check fraud and bribery, and conspiracy to defraud the government. No real assessment of the amount of loss in funds to the government and the taxpayer could be made, but many post offices were loaded with worthless or inferior mechanical devices that had been sold to the government at a profit to key federal employees in Washington. One of the best descriptions of the frauds was written by William Allen White for *McClure's Magazine*. White had encouraged President Roosevelt to make the investigation and had assisted Bristow in securing information in some of the scandals.[57]

Roosevelt wrote a public letter to Payne congratulating him on the success of the investigation and the credit it had brought to the government. Payne, in turn, commended Bristow and his inspectors for their zeal, vigor, and fidelity in the investigation. Roosevelt's public letter, however, did not satisfy the reform element, which insisted that the President's chief politician, Payne, must be dismissed.[58] On October 3, 1903, Bonaparte wrote to Conrad that President Roosevelt was omitting the names of the congressmen involved in the scandals from the published report of Bristow's findings. Bonaparte felt that such a course was open to "very serious objection."[59] Both Bonaparte and Conrad declared that the congressmen had acted illegally and the President was obligated to report any breach of trust. Payne and Bristow did not follow this recommendation.

Meanwhile, reasons for the suppression of parts of Bristow's report were whispered about Washington. Party leaders and congressmen close to the President were reported to be involved.[60] Bristow had information on 900 cases involving 150 congressmen who had pressed for unwarranted rentals and salaries, and Roosevelt, shocked at the number of cases in which congressmen were involved, ordered Payne to cancel the increases in rentals and salaries. The House Committee on Post Offices and Post Roads, alarmed at the charges and the cancellations, requested the papers from Payne for investigation. Payne called upon Bristow for a complete list. Bristow was ill from January 25 to March 14, and the chief of the postal inspectors drew up the final list with abstracts on each case. At first Payne withheld the names on the list, but he later sent them at the request of the House committee.[61] Once again the press was in its glory. Bristow, Payne, and Roosevelt were accused by the named congressmen of blackening their reputations, as well as that of the sacred body of the nation's lawmakers. Bristow naturally received the bulk of these accusations. It was demanded that he be removed from office and resolutions of censure prepared. A special congressional committee appointed to make an investigation soon whitewashed the charges against its fellow members, and the resolutions of censure were dropped.[62]

By the end of March, 1904, Bristow's work was finished. In spite of a careful investigation, there was not enough evidence to prosecute Perry Heath. The trials of the offenders continued until the spring of 1905. Several of the conspirators were found guilty, fined, and given penitentiary sentences. The investigation implicated former congressmen, as well as Post Office Department employees. Machen, the chief conspirator and one of the most influential men in Washington, was fined $10,000 and sentenced to two years in prison. Several of Machen's business associates received the same punishment.[63]

Almost by accident the investigation led to the conviction of Senator Joseph R. Burton, from Abilene, Kansas. Burton was found guilty of accepting pay from the Rialto Grain and Securities Company of St. Louis for interceding with postal authorities to render a favorable decision in the company's use of the mails. Burton was fined $2,500 and sentenced to six months in prison. After losing an appeal before the Supreme Court, Burton resigned his seat in the Senate on June 4, 1906.[64] The Burton faction in Kansas politics accused Bristow of prosecuting Burton in order to win the latter's seat at Washington. Although the accusations were groundless, they served as a deterrent to Bristow's political advancement in later years.

The impact of the postal investigations was highly advantageous to Roosevelt's administration. At first the President and Postmaster-General Payne had been accused of fraud and corruption, but the investigation showed that the chief offenders had been selected by the previous administration. Roosevelt's quick action in ordering the investigation and the fact that congressmen had been accused of wrongdoing raised the executive branch in public esteem and smoothed the way for Roosevelt's nomination in 1904. Bristow won a public acclaim for his thoroughness, and in Kansas he was, for a time, the state's most prominent man. The investigation had demonstrated the need for a return to the early demands of the civil service reformers for more businesslike practices in the conduct of the affairs of the nation. Congressmen could not risk a hostile public opinion, and in April, 1904, the office of purchasing agent for the Post Office Department was established. Although it was handicapped by a limited clerical force, the new agency in its first year reported a saving of $218,296.64 through centralized purchases.[65] Both Bristow and Payne continued to work for an improved postal service. However, administrative changes soon brought trouble for Bristow.

Postmaster-General Payne died on October 4, 1904. The first assistant, Robert Wynne, was elevated to Payne's position, with the understanding that, if the Roosevelt administration were returned to Washington, George B. Cortelyou, chairman of the Republican National Committee, would take over in March, 1905. Wynne was one of the few career men who had been chosen for a cabinet position. In the eyes of the public, postal affairs had been placed in good hands, and all seemed quiet in the department. But Washington, as well as the nation, was shocked when the Washington *Post* announced that Bristow had resigned from the postal service on January 13, 1905.

Bristow's resignation had come as a bitter and earnest protest against Wynne's decision to move the force of postal inspectors and the division of mail depredations from Bristow's jurisdiction to the Postmaster-General's own office. This meant that Bristow would lose over two hundred of his staff and some of the most effective men in his department. Many of the inspectors were Bristow's most trusted friends. Bristow declared that Wynne had acted unfairly and had secured President Roosevelt's approval for the order prior to a complete statement on the situation. Wynne immediately denied that he had acted too quickly and insisted that the move was for the good of the entire service. Bristow held two hurried conferences with President Roosevelt, but the transfer ordered was not rescinded.

There was little doubt that congressmen who had to deal with Bristow, especially those whose names had appeared in the postal investigation, had pressed Roosevelt to drop Bristow.[66] Postal records in the National Archives show that both Payne and Bristow had been firm with members of the Senate and the House of Representatives. There is ample evidence that often, after Bristow had sent inspectors to investigate postmasters against whom congressmen had made charges, the department had refused to make the requested removals.[67] Congressmen who felt that it was their right to change postmasters clamored for Bristow's dismissal, and Roosevelt gave in to the pressure. The removal of the inspection staff from Bristow's jurisdiction made his position untenable.

William Allen White wrote to Bristow that he knew the fourth assistant postmaster-general had been treated "in a most dastardly manner."[68]

The editor of the Topeka *Journal* wrote that for eight years there had hardly been a government official "who has been in the public gaze more than Bristow."[69] He described Bristow as one whose way was set with snares, "most of which he eluded." According to the editor, Bristow was honest, courageous, relentless, and his "pathway was strewn with deeds accomplished and wrecks of dishonest men in public service whom he had pursued successfully." Kansas Senator Chester Long was quoted in the *Journal* editorial as saying, "the way of the transgressor is hard; I say the way of the investigator is harder." Later, in 1908, White wrote that the trouble with Bristow was that "he went against the buzz saw . . . . He did his duty and more and got the worst of it for his work."[70] The best account of Bristow's resignation was written by Charles Dawes in his journal entry on July 12, 1905:

My old friend, J. L. Bristow, formerly 4th Assistant Postmaster General, . . . visited me and spent several hours. He is on his way home to Kansas to take up his little country newspaper work again, after having done his country great service in great things.

He says Roosevelt has cast him ruthlessly aside after listening to the enemies against whom he had faithfully promised to protect him, when he appointed him to the work of running down some thieves. He said that he realized it would only injure him to express himself publicly as to the way he had been treated by Roosevelt and, therefore, would keep silent.

Bristow maintained that, in his friendships and personal relations, Roosevelt is insincere, subordinating all matters of personal loyalty or rights of an individual (providing he be weak or too obscure to become a martyr in the public eye) to his own ambitions and interests. He says that his friendships are largely artificial, being based on self interest—chiefly that he either overpraises or overcondemns—and that his desire for public applause overrides his desire to give a weak man a square deal. In this I find Secretary Gage agrees with Bristow—in fact I suspect Roosevelt makes a hard man to work under.[71]

The eight years as a postal administrator had been valuable to Bristow, even though they had come to an abrupt and unhappy ending. He had enjoyed the administrative work, and it had matured him for a public career that was still over the political horizon. Friends, including White and Senator Long, pressed Roosevelt to find a new position for Bristow. Perhaps the President realized that he must not lose the services of a valuable party man; he quickly appointed Bristow as a special commissioner to the Panama Railroad Company.

4

Panama Ventures

Joseph Bristow's resignation from his position as fourth assistant postmaster-general became effective on January 20, 1905. That was indeed a busy and critical time for President Roosevelt, who, by the landslide in the election of 1904, had become President in his own right. Diplomatic affairs were strained and cloudy, and domestic issues were pressing. Roosevelt was then working on his inaugural message, selecting a new cabinet, and lining up congressional support for his domestic program. Had Bristow chosen to make an open break with the administration, he could have caused Roosevelt some public embarrassment. The newspapers played up the idea that the President had placed Bristow in a more significant and remunerative position. The special commissioner to the Panama Railroad Company would receive $15.00 a day plus all traveling expenses, and he was provided a secretary who was on the government payroll. Bristow's friends who were close to the administration were not fooled by this publicity, for they knew that the new position would be of a temporary nature. They could also see that Bristow's associates in the Post Office Department were being shifted rapidly to new positions. Postmaster-General Wynne was trying desperately to free himself from Bristow's influence.[1]

Bristow's new appointment could not, however, be regarded as an unnecessary one. Soon after William H. Taft became Secretary of War, President Roosevelt had given him the supervision of the affairs in the Philippine Islands, and Congress had added the supervision of the Panama Canal to his duties. Either assignment would have been a full-time job. The supervision of both areas rapidly drained Taft's energies, and he needed Bristow's assistance in railroad matters in Panama.

There had been great haste on the part of the Roosevelt administration to acquire the right to build a canal across the Isthmus of Panama, but by January, 1905, affairs were dragging. The editors across the land were crying for the "dirt to fly." But Taft was surrounded by many embarrassing pressures and problems. He had visited the Canal Zone with a group of engineers in November, 1904, and had recognized the difficulty of the task ahead. He was aware of the sanitation and health problem and of the need for good roads, a communication system, and harbor installations. He was faced with the problem of finding competent engineers, and he had to assure the Panamanians that they would secure a share of the profits from the business the canal would bring to the area. At first Taft supported the idea of a sea-level canal, but he swung to Roosevelt's support when the latter decided in May, 1905, that a lock canal would be cheaper to build and could be completed sooner than a sea-level ditch.[2]

Every phase of activity in the Canal Zone was made more delicate by the fact that a corporation owned by the government of the United States was to build and operate the canal. Congressmen were hostile to this nearly socialistic venture. Railroad interests, already under the threat of more governmental regulation, were openly hostile to the government-owned canal project, and owners of steamship lines were demanding an entree to the new business venture. Taft had to examine all the complaints and, in a sense, walk a tight rope. As a special commissioner, Bristow was

Joseph Bristow in His Later Years

Salina in the 1920's; *Journal* Building in Background
Kansas State Historical Society

Irrigating Pond, Saunders County, Nebraska, about 1898

to deal directly with Secretary Taft, but he had to reflect the desires of President Roosevelt as well.

Bristow's assignment was extensive and there was little time for his own preparation. His special task was to appraise the Panama Railroad Company, to examine the complaints against its practices, and to determine the best policy to be pursued by the government in the management of the company. In addition he was to visit Atlantic ports, Gulf ports, and Pacific ports to investigate trade opportunities and freight rates in these areas. And he was to consider trade opportunities farther afield with distant South American countries and with European countries.[3]

The railroad across the Isthmus of Panama had been completed in the mid-1850's. It was an extremely profitable venture. When the French company started to build a canal, it purchased 68 per cent of the railroad stock. This stock became the property of the United States when the government purchased the French canal holdings. The firm of Sullivan and Cromwell served as legal counsel to the Panama Railroad Company, and William Cromwell was directed by the Isthmian Canal Commission to purchase the remainder of the railroad stock. He completed this transaction early in 1905 and turned 728 shares, costing $73,437.49, over to Secretary Taft.[4] Taft had received many complaints against the operation of the railroad: it was monopolistic, its equipment was run down, the passenger and freight rates were excessive, it operated a near monopoly with steamships in the Atlantic Ocean and had a special contract with the Pacific Mail Steamship Company which granted this firm a monopoly in the Pacific Ocean. The railroad's contracts with Central and South American steamship companies also operated on a near-monopoly basis. Other complaints were that freight was handled carelessly and that commercial business was given a secondary position to canal business.[5]

In a few days Bristow hurriedly briefed himself on the main complaints and gathered as many facts on the conditions in Panama as time allowed. With the aid of his secretary, he prepared questionnaires for mailing to rail, steamship, and business interests that were involved in trade through the Panama route.

Bristow's first stop was at the offices of the Panama Railroad Company in New York City, where he examined the financial and shipping records of the company and left an extensive questionnaire with E. A. Drake, the vice-president and secretary of the company. On February 7, 1905, Bristow sailed for Panama on the steamship *Advance*. He spent ten days with H. G. Prescott, the acting superintendent of the railroad, examining the properties held by the company and discussing the problems of supervision and management. He also conferred with John W. Wallace, chief engineer of the Canal Commission, and with Major General George W. Davis, governor of the Canal Zone. Bristow soon learned that the railroad was the most vital factor in the early stages of the canal project. The French company had allowed the road and harbor facilities to deteriorate, and it was necessary to rebuild them before any serious work could be done on the canal itself.

On February 23, Bristow sailed north from Panama on the steamship *City of Panama*. He visited seaports in Costa Rica, Nicaragua, El Salvador, and Guatemala, landing at Salina Cruz, Mexico, on March 5. He examined the harbor facilities that were being built by the Mexican government on the Isthmus of Tehuantepec and consulted with Mexican officials who were building the Tehuantepec National Railway from Salina Cruz to Coatzacoalcos. Bristow then sailed to Veracruz and traveled by rail to Mexico City, where he called on President Porfirio Díaz. From Mexico City he went to the Pacific coast, visiting San Diego, Los Angeles, San Francisco, Portland, Tacoma, and Seattle.[6] From Los Angeles, Bristow reported that his Panama trip had been well worthwhile and added, "I am well fortified with many facts to lay before the President."[7] On the West Coast tour he interviewed chamber of commerce representatives, bankers, businessmen, and rail and steamship officials to gather material on freight rates, shipping routes, and future trade needs of the Panama route. He also secured information from his questionnaires and correspondence with consuls and consular agents.

From Seattle, Bristow returned to Washington and conferred with Secretary Taft, who suggested that he should visit the Gulf ports of Pensacola, Mobile, New Orleans, and Galveston before he completed his report. After a short excursion to the Gulf ports in April, Bristow returned to Washington to complete the writing of his official report; it was made public on July 10, 1905.[8]

The report was detailed and thorough in a typical Bristow manner. Ever aware of congressional hostility to the governmental ownership and operation of the Panama Railroad Company, Bristow nevertheless recommended that the government ownership and operation should be continued and declared that the Panama investment was "pure 18K gold." He reviewed the history of the road in Panama and gave a detailed account of the operating conditions and the economic values of the company property. He described the health and labor problems and enumerated the business holdings that the company owned and operated in the Canal Zone, with special emphasis on the harbor facilities.

In spite of the immense strain that the company had to face in the actual building of the canal, Bristow recommended that the railroad should be continued as a commercial line. He urged that the road facilities be improved at once with better roadbeds and heavier rails and rolling stock and that some thirty-seven miles of the original road be double-tracked. He recommended expanded harbor facilities and efforts to build up new trade that could be directed to the Canal Zone, during the several years before the canal could be completed. The steamship line operated by the Panama Railroad Company between New York and Colón should be continued and its carrying capacity increased.

Bristow felt that shipping conditions on the West Coast were very unsatisfactory and that the shipping rates were excessive. Shippers and exporters on the coast were apparently in a very touchy position; they did not wish to be too critical of the Pacific Mail and Steamship Company for fear that the railroad would retaliate against them. The Pacific Mail line was not trying to develop the coastal trade to the Panama route, however, and Bristow recommended that the contracts of the Panama Railroad Company with this line and with South American lines be canceled.

As for the Gulf ports, Bristow pointed out that they had never had facilities for trade via the Panama route with the west coast of North and South America. He reported that when the Panama Railroad Company had chartered a steamship to operate between New Orleans and Colón, the Southern Pacific Railroad Company had immediately cut its rates on goods that might be shipped by the Panama route. The merchants in New Orleans deserted the steamship line and returned to the use of the railroad. When the ocean operation was discontinued, the railroad rates were greatly increased. To aid the Gulf ports, Bristow recommended that, if a private steamship line were not opened from the Gulf to Panama, the Panama Railroad Company should be directed to open such a line.

Bristow stated that the new shipping rates that the Panama Railroad Company had established on February 1, 1905, were reasonable, and closed his report by urging that American shipping interests should be favored in future trade through the Canal Zone in so far as it was possible under the existing treaty obligations of the United States.[9]

Bristow's report served as a guide for President Roosevelt and Secretary Taft, as well as for the Isthmian Commission. It was also pleasing to the progressives in Congress, who were girding themselves for a showdown fight to control railway rates and abuses at home. Privately owned railroad companies would not be allowed to gouge the government in the construction of the canal. Although making only a small profit for the government, the Panama Railroad Company would render a vital service.

In April, 1905, the headquarters of the Isthmian Commission were moved from Washington to the Canal Zone. The authorities immediately decided to use the railroad as an adjunct to the canal. The old road was completely overhauled, and thirty-seven miles were double-tracked. Many miles of track for construction trains and spoils trains, which were used for hauling away rock and waste material, were laid. Cargo docks, piers, and harbors were increased in size, and enormous terminal facilities and business and living quarters were erected. In 1904, during the early digging of the canal, the railroad handled 17,000,000 ton miles, but by 1909–10 the road handled over 300,000,000 ton miles. In 1912–13 a new railroad was constructed on the east side of the canal above the water level of the lakes; but the old road, patterned along Bristow's recommendations, had carried the largest share of the canal-construction load, and it had kept commercial service open as well.[10]

Bristow received considerable publicity while he was making his survey. In March it was rumored that he might be given a place on the Isthmian Commission.[11] In June, Senator Chester Long of Kansas pressed Secretary Taft to transfer one of the commission's members to the engineering staff in order to make a place for Bristow. Long wrote Taft, "I have a letter from the President in which he says he will do anything he can for Mr. Bristow, but of course, I know that the arrangement of the matter will ultimately devolve on you." He added, "The appointment of Mr. Bristow will not only properly recognize the merit of a deserving official, but will be very much appreciated in Kansas by the President's friends and be a special favor to me."[12]

The appointment did not materialize, and Bristow announced late in July, 1905, that he was returning to Kansas to manage his newspaper business. There were many rumors to the effect that Bristow was retiring permanently from public life, but from the middle of 1905, Bristow's name was constantly before the public.[13] The editor of the Topeka *State Journal* on August 18, 1905, urged that "Joe" should take Senator Burton's place in Washington. But Burton, who had been convicted and sentenced for receiving illegal compensation from a private company, carried his case to the United States Supreme Court and did not resign his seat in the Senate until June 4, 1906. At that time the liberal Republicans pressed Governor Hoch to select Bristow, but the position was finally given to Alfred W. Benson, a Republican lawyer and district court judge from Ottawa, Kansas. In 1907, Burton purchased the Salina *Daily Union* and became one of Bristow's business competitors.[14]

Whatever desires Bristow might have had to return to Washington, he could not sit on the political sidelines and wait for an opening. He had a growing family to support and a newspaper that had suffered from his absence. The family returned to Salina, and Bristow settled down to revamp the *Evening Journal,* turning it into one of the better small-town newspapers in the state.

Bristow's name appeared as editor on the September 1, 1905, issue. He pointed out to the readers that new presses had been purchased and that they would operate with huge rolls of newsprint purchased by the carload. The new type did improve the newspaper's appearance. The published circulation for October, 1905 was 1,659. The *Evening Journal* offered a wide coverage of national and international affairs, as well as of state and local news, especially in reporting church, school, and college affairs. On September 20, Bristow wrote a penetrating editorial on the need for greater material rewards in the teaching profession in order to attract bright young people to it. The tone of the editorial was decidedly progressive. Senator Jonathan Dolliver of Iowa, who was gradually moving to the support of progressive issues, had spoken at the Chautauqua in Salina during the summer, and Bristow declared the speech to be one of the highlights of the year.

Over and over Bristow hit at the current railroad abuses, furnishing ample statistics on the long- and short-haul problems. He insisted that Kansas did not want socialism, but unless the railway commission was freed from railroad control, Kansas citizens would be forced to welcome "Socialists and Demagogues" as preferable to a "condition of continued and determined injustice." Ample space was given to President Roosevelt's speech on the need for rate regulation delivered at Richmond, Virginia, on October 19, 1905. Constantly, Bristow's *Evening Journal* spread the liberal doctrines of the day. The merits of conservation, primary elections, rural free delivery, and independent voting were carefully detailed. At the same time vigorous opposition was given to the corrupt practices of insurance companies and to corporation contributions to campaign funds. The readers of the *Evening Journal* could put Bristow clearly on the liberal side of his party; if he had a political future, it lay clearly along the path of progressivism. On August 29, 1905, Bristow endorsed Taft as President Roosevelt's successor, and he busied himself with Republican activities in the state.

Meanwhile, his business interests grew. Bristow was offered the opportunity to purchase the Wichita *Beacon*[15]. Although he decided not to take on that financial obligation, his business associate, Henry J. Allen, decided to take the plunge. The purchase price was approximately $90,000. The transaction was completed on February 28, 1907, when Allen took over the editorship from H. J. Hagney.[16] Bristow, in turn, became sole owner of the Salina *Evening Journal* and the Journal building. This was a heavy financial commitment for Bristow, one which he paid off in monthly installments of $200 over a long period of years.

When Bristow returned to Kansas, he believed that his connections with problems in Panama had ended. As an editor he watched and reported on the construction of the canal, but he had no idea that his services might be sought again by Secretary Taft. Taft spoke at Ottawa on June 20, 1907; over eight thousand people heard his Chautauqua address on the Panama Canal. At a banquet in the Elsmere Boarding House, Bristow sat with Taft and other Republican leaders including Long, Curtis, Mulvane, Harris, and Stubbs.[17] Commercial matters between the Pacific coastal towns and the Canal Zone were still unsettled, and on August 27, 1907, Secretary Taft asked Bristow for further assistance.

Taft wrote that the service by the Pacific Mail had "become so utterly unsatisfactory that we are getting no business at all for loading out ships at Colon for New York." Taft was seriously considering asking President Roosevelt to recommend the purchase by the Isthmian Commission of "four or five" steamships adapted for trade between Pacific ports and Panama. He asked Bristow to serve again as a special railroad commissioner and to make a full report by December 12, 1907.[18] On September 4, Taft authorized Bristow to visit New York and San Francisco to secure necessary data in regard to the steamship service on the Pacific. "I hope," Taft wrote, "that you will make the expense as low as possible."[19] C. C. Wagner, Taft's private secretary, provided Bristow with stationery and made early appointments for Bristow on his new assignment.[20]

Bristow's reaction to Taft's new request was shown in a letter to E. A. Drake of the Panama Railroad Company. "I was surprised at receiving this request from Secretary Taft," wrote Bristow. "I have been attending my private business for two years and have had a most delightful rest and recreation, but I am anxious to be of any service to the Secretary that I can in connection with any of the perplexing questions that he has before him for consideration."[21] Drake replied on September 23, 1907, with a discouraging note, that in view of the "unsatisfactory results of our efforts to operate" a steamship line between Panama and San Francisco, "only a courageous official would assume the responsibility of advising the Government to engage in so hazardous an undertaking, as it is very doubtful if Congress and 'the public' would sanction the venture, judging from the intermittent opposition to the operation for Government account of the existing Panama Rail Road Steamship Line."[22] One of Drake's secretaries, P. H. Cahill, wrote to Bristow that "Secretary Taft has shown good judgment, and I am so glad he has succeeded in routing you from your Kansas hermitage."[23]

The second investigation was not as time-consuming as the first had been in 1905. Bristow drafted a one-page questionnaire which he sent to commercial and business interests on the West Coast. He also renewed his correspondence with business leaders and representatives of chambers of commerce on both East and West Coasts. He found that shipping problems of the Panama route had changed little since 1905 and that the Pacific Mail Steamship Company was rendering still less service than it had during his previous investigation, in spite of a great increase in oceanic shipping in Pacific waters. Many businessmen on the

West Coast were anxious to sell supplies to the government for the construction of the Panama Canal. Business leaders in Portland, Seattle, Tacoma, San Francisco, San Diego, and even Honolulu were eager for direct shipping connections with the Canal Zone, although the merchants of Los Angeles, the chief stopping point of Pacific Mail, had little interest in any change. J. S. Ackerman, who represented the San Diego Chamber of Commerce, wrote to Bristow that no one in southern California "believes the Pacific Mail is anything but a side issue of the Southern Pacific and no one here expects the Pacific Mail to do anything but play into the hands of the Southern Pacific under its present control."[24] Ackerman's complaint was typical of many others that Bristow received.

Bristow visited New York and Washington and completed his report to Secretary Taft on schedule. The report was confidential and was not made public until Bristow appeared before the Senate Committee on Interoceanic Canals in January of 1908. The public report was dated January 20, 1908.[25]

In the report Bristow reviewed the recommendations he had made in 1905 and presented a detailed account of the rail and terminal facilities that had been built after his first report. He then described the government-operated rail and shipping lines and their influence in holding down the rates charged by private steamship companies operating in the Atlantic. Bristow reported that all the evidence he could find strongly favored the establishment of a government-operated steamship line in the Pacific. He used three basic arguments for his proposal: first, that the new line could promptly and efficiently transfer men and materials from the west-coast cities for the construction of the Panama Canal; second, that a government-operated line was essential to keep open the Panama route which had been in existence for over fifty years; third, that such a line would provide adequate cargo for the Panama Railroad Company's steamships eastward bound from Colón.

Congress took no action on Bristow's proposal. Beyond a doubt, Drake had correctly predicted congressional hostility to the government-owned steamship lines. Although the results of this report were not as direct as those of his first survey, Bristow's second investigation was not without merit. It showed the vise-like grip that railroads had on the American transportation system and the need for protection of public interests. Before publication of Bristow's first report, William Allen White had urged George Lorimer of the *Saturday Evening Post* to report Bristow's findings. White wrote to Lorimer, "It is a big vital thing in the way the Government is going to run it [the Panama Railroad] to break transcontinental freight rate and you ought to have it."[26] The second investigation, in turn, made the public aware that President Roosevelt and Secretary Taft had not dropped the drive for fair and just rates.

For Bristow, who had by now entered the Kansas primary election for a seat in the United States Senate, the report was one more item of proof to the public of how he stood on the railroad rate problem, and it was additional evidence that he had the confidence of Secretary Taft, who was now actively campaigning to become President Roosevelt's successor. Nor was the idea of a government-owned steamship line in the Pacific completely forgotten: After Bristow entered the Senate he again explored the possibility of establishing such a project. Bristow's Panama ventures had enabled him to become well informed on the construction and transportation problems involved in the building of the Panama Canal. As a senator he was prepared to make valuable contributions toward the successful completion and operation of the canal.

5

The Senatorial Campaign

The progressive winds that swept across the nation in the first decade of the 1900's deeply influenced the political scene in the Midwest. Politics became more than mere factional struggle for power and patronage. The idea of human welfare had entered into politics, and there were demands at both state and national levels that legislative bodies must consider the common good before partisanship. The feeling was current that the average man had been neglected far too long in favor of the vested interests, and the foundations of the party structures were frequently shaken by attacks against such existing political machinery as the selection of United State senators by state legislators. Slowly the tools by which governmental bodies could be made more responsive to public demands were given to the voters.

Many Kansas voters were caught in the new political currents, and a new leadership began to battle the old guard for control of the Republican party. Businessmen, farmers, and professional men were filled with the spirit of reform, and many editors in the state proclaimed the new political doctrines of the day. William Allen White, Walter Roscoe Stubbs, Joseph Bristow, Arthur Capper, Victor Murdock, Henry Allen, Edmond H. Madison, and a host of others had fallen under the spell of Theodore Roosevelt, whose sudden rise to the Presidency brought forth the promise of a square deal and justice for all. "Teddy" had toured Kansas before the Republican convention in 1900. In Chicago the Kansas delegation had visited Roosevelt and pledged itself to his nomination for the Vice-Presidency. Even the cynical Joseph Cannon credited the Kansas delegation with Roosevelt's nomination. Roosevelt kept Kansas on his touring schedule and made many friends in the state, and Kansans were elated when, in 1904, Roosevelt was nominated for the Presidency.[1] It was a period marked by high optimism, good times, good crops, and a crusading zeal.

Prominent Republicans toured Kansas. Beginning in 1902, Albert B. Cummins of Iowa paid three annual visits to his neighboring state, and Jonathan Dolliver, also from Iowa, made political tours in 1904 and 1908 in Kansas.[2] Robert LaFollette and William Borah joined the pilgrimage to the Sunflower State. Through a friendly local press and from the Chautauqua platforms of many towns in Kansas, these men filled the air with the "Iowa Idea," the "Wisconsin Plan," the program of U'Ren in Oregon, and the best fruits of Populism. So electric was the demand for reform that the aged former Senator William A. Peffer declared in June of 1907 that "the country now hotly demands legislation it abused me for advocating."[3] And a young editor of the Topeka *Capital,* Arthur Capper, wrote, "What Wisconsin did, Kansas can do." Capper demanded that the people emancipate the state from corporation domination and urged the adoption of the direct primary, the establishment of a railway commission, and the abolition of the free-pass evil.[4]

The struggle for the control of the Republican party in the state was well illustrated in the rise of Walter Roscoe Stubbs, so aptly described by the New York *Sun* as "an optimist run by a high powered dynamo." Stubbs, a contractor, had made part of his fortune building grades for railroad companies. He was a dynamic man, physically towering a head higher than most men, always ready for a good political ruckus. He entered the state legislature in 1903 and was elected governor in 1908; no man in the history of the state had become so prominent a figure in so short a time. At this period he was, beyond a doubt, the most potent single factor in the public life of Kansas, and he had ample support from Capper, Bristow, White, and Murdock. In 1904, Stubbs helped form the Boss Busters, a group of liberal legislators. They selected Edward W. Hoch as their candidate for governor and defeated Governor Willis J. Bailey in his bid for a second term. In July, 1906, leading Republicans, under Stubbs's direction, gathered in Topeka and formed the Square Dealers, electing J. A. Troutman permanent chairman and Arthur Capper secretary. Immediate steps were taken to raise funds to fight railroad influence in the state, and petitions were sent to all Republican candidates for office asking them to pledge their support for a state primary election law. Stubbs, who always had a large amount of money to spend on public causes, started the fund with a five-hundred-dollar contribution. The railroad fight was declared to be national as well as state.[5]

Stubbs, the firebrand from Lawrence, created consternation within the ranks of the old guard. Cyrus Leland, Morton Albaugh, and David Mulvane, all conservatives, struck back at the liberal wing of the party. Stubbs could control the legislature and the governorship, but he could not get the United States senatorship under his thumb. Here the conservatives held firm, and after the election in 1902, Leland and Albaugh dictated the selection of Chester Long for United States senator. The power of the railroads was felt in Long's selection. Although the Rock Island men supported Long's fellow congressman, Charles Curtis, the support given Long by the Santa Fe and the Missouri Pacific was decisive. The conservatives agreed that Curtis would have Long's support for the next Senate vacancy, which would occur in 1906.[6] However, Bristow and several other leading Republicans had their eyes on the seat that the railroad interests had promised to Curtis for 1906.

When Bristow resigned the postal service in 1905, he confided in a private letter to Senator Long that he hoped to return to the Senate and work with Long. In his disappointment with Theodore Roosevelt, whom he had first so much admired, he expressed a hope that he and Long could do some "big-sticking" against the White House incumbent. This letter was later printed in the Kansas City *Journal,* on July 15, 1908, and it was to cause Bristow some difficulty. While Bristow's ambition was known among his close friends, he did not publicly enter the Senate race until May, 1906. Bristow had hoped for Long's support, but Long's advisers felt that Bristow would never make friends with the average Kansan; he was described as too cold. Gradually the Long forces moved to the support of the incumbent congressman, Charles Curtis.[7] William Allen White rallied to the support of Bristow and the Stubbs forces. White brought LaFollette to the state in 1906, hoping to put a freeze on Long, and LaFollette pressed Bristow's cause publicly and privately on his speaking tour.[8] Bristow realized, however, that he would need to stage a statewide fight against the railroads and the corporations to defeat the Curtis faction, and he did not choose to use such campaign tactics.[9]

When the newly elected legislature met to choose the next senator, in January, 1907, eight men were nominated on the floor of the legislature for the seat in the Senate. Former Governor Bailey, Murdock, and Stubbs were among the men running against Curtis and Bristow. Curtis was selected on the fourth ballot. Only four state senators and ten representatives stayed with Bristow. It was probably little consolation for Bristow when White wrote to him on January 17, "If Kansas has lost a good Senator it has at least gained a brave editor."[10]

The outcome of the senatorial contest in the state legislature was ample proof to Stubbs, Bristow, Murdock, and many other liberals that the power of the old guard in the Republican party could not be curbed until Kansas adopted a primary-election law. The need for such a law had been advocated since the early days of the Populists, but it took many years for the idea to win public support. Senator John Chaney introduced a primary bill in 1901, but his proposal was easily defeated. The Boss Busters forced a primary plank into the Republican platform in 1904, and Curtis endorsed the idea in 1905. Senator Long opposed the plank, arguing that the party primary would be hard to supervise and that the party could not pay a candidate's financial expenses in a primary election. Long feared that his party faction would lose support in the western part of the state, where Bristow had strong support. The Square Dealers had tried in 1906 to get all Republican candidates to endorse the primary plank, but Long ignored the request.[11]

At first Bristow was hesitant about endorsing the idea of a direct primary election; he wrote and spoke about the concept of a weighted ballot in the primary contests. But by September, 1906, he was solidly backing the proposal to cover all candidates, including United States senators. He led the Saline County drive for a state-wide primary, and soon his proposal was getting wide acceptance in the western part of the state.

Governor Hoch had promised that he would work hard for a primary bill, and Stubbs pushed a bill in 1907. But the liberals again saw defeat by the old-guard supporters of the party convention. Governor Hoch remained true to his promise, however; he issued a call for a special session of the legislature, to convene on January 16, 1908, and during the session he asked the legislature for a primary law, a bank-deposit law, and amendments to the new tax law. At this time Long, following the advice of his supporters, endorsed the primary proposal.

The special session gave the state its first primary-election law, but the legislation did not represent an absolute victory for the liberals. The new law provided that all candidates for state and national offices were to be nominated in primary elections, but the party candidate for the United States Senate had to carry a majority of the representative and senatorial districts in the state. If such a nomination was won, the legislators were pledged to send the candidate to the Senate.[12]

The new primary law enabled the liberal wing of the Republican party to get the names of its candidates before the voters of the state, and it was clear that this was the only means by which Joseph Bristow could win the senatorial contest in 1908. As early as February 3, 1908, White wrote to Long, "Of course you know Joe is going to run for Senator. He has not asked my advice in the matter, but probably will have my support."[13] Bristow announced on February 15 that he would be a candidate against Long, and in a few days White was working for Bristow and Stubbs, who had filed for governor in response to White's editorial efforts to draft him. Long wrote to a friend, W. S. Fitzpatrick, that he was confident of winning the battle, but that he did not "underestimate" the extent of the opposition because he had not "been as radical" as some thought he should be.[14]

Bristow's primary campaign against Long became the most spectacular contest in the state. Both men had good national reputations, and each had his supporters among national party leaders. Long's career in the House and Senate enabled him to claim that he had supported the national platform and had administration support. Bristow, likewise, had enjoyed a national reputation as fourth assistant postmaster-general, and he had been one of the first to endorse Secretary Taft as President Roosevelt's successor. It was nearly a year after Bristow's endorsement of Taft that Roosevelt had written to White that Taft would "make an ideal President." Neither Taft nor Roosevelt could take sides, but the President knew that Bristow was closer than Long to progressive issues.

At the state level Long held an advantageous position. It is always difficult to dislodge a senator in Kansas. The Kansas City *Star* and the Topeka *Capital,* both with extensive coverage, had supported Long's work. Long had ample funds of his own, as well as liberal contributions from his friends for conducting his campaign. Long, also, had Morton Albaugh for a campaign manager and W. Y. Morgan of Hutchinson for a literary agent; both men were established party leaders. Bristow had little money, and he had been moving to the left of the party leadership in order to advance his case. In a letter to F. M. Hartman, who had solicited advertising space for his Frankfort paper, Bristow wrote: "I

Typical Chautauqua Crowd, Ottawa, Kansas
Kansas State Historical Society

Edmund Morrill,
Governor of Kansas, 1895-96
Kansas State Historical Society

John Harrison,
Bristow's Chief Postal Inspector
Kansas State Historical Society

Charles Curtis, Vice-President
during Hoover Administration
Kansas State Historical Society

William Allen White,
Emporia *Gazette* Editor

Arthur Capper,
Governor of Kansas, 1915-19
Kansas State Historical Society

Roy F. Bailey, Bristow's Manager
and Editor of Salina *Journal*
Kansas State Historical Society

beg to state that my financial resources are such that I am unable to take advertising in newspapers throughout the state. I appreciate very much the cordial support that the newspaper boys are giving me. The only money I have spent in the campaign is the money earned in the publication of a country daily and you know that is not very much for such a campaign as I have been making. Indeed, it is very meagre."[15]

Bristow did have a genuine advantage in the assistance of William Allen White, who served as literary spokesman and marshaled newspaper and financial support for Bristow's campaign. White sought funds from many sources. On May 13, 1908, he asked for a loan from former Governor Morrill.[16] When word of the request leaked out, White declared that his action had been proper: "Mr. Bristow is a poor man and has no money." According to White, Bristow lived "frugally and would save money on his salary." There was no reason why he "shouldn't borrow whatever money he could."[17] On July 1, 1908, White wrote Robert LaFollette, "Poor Joe Bristow! hasn't got a dollar in the world and is making this fight on his nerve against a powerful machine, and against all the railroad money that can be used."[18]

The Topeka *State Journal* on June 9, 1908, declared that Bristow had no manager, but made his own campaign plans, arranged his own dates, and dictated his own letters. Bristow did have excellent help, however, from the staff of the Salina *Evening Journal,* in which his campaign material was printed. Bristow's oldest son, Joseph Q., served as editor of the campaign literature and as business manager. His second son, Frank, gathered news for the *Journal* whenever, as his father in a lighter moment declared, they could get Frank out of bed. Young Ed, a student at Kansas Wesleyan, helped to organize the faculty and student body at the university.

Bristow's platform called for revising the tariff, limiting the amount of stocks and bonds that could be issued by a corporation engaged in interstate business, prohibiting gambling in stocks and grain futures, enlarging the powers of the Interstate Commerce Commission to determine the costs and value of railroads, safeguarding the state's authority over interstate business, and restricting the sale of coal lands belonging to the United States. The platform announcement closed with this statement: "I am a progressive Republican and in the politics of the country stand with Roosevelt, Taft, LaFollette and Hughes and the ideas they represent."[19]

White wrote over one thousand letters in behalf of Bristow, and he secured space in the Kansas City *Star* and the Topeka *Capital* for his cause. Through the columns of the Emporia *Gazette* he condemned the Albaugh-Morgan-Leland machine and branded Long as a railroad and big business senator and a follower of Senator Aldrich and Speaker Cannon.[20] Two of White's accounts were highly effective. In "The Case of Mr. Bristow," White branded Long as an alien and declared that, although Bristow was undeniably "cold," Long could not even speak the Kansas language and used "Billy" Morgan as his chief interpreter with "Mort" Albaugh translating the "high Kansas" of Morgan into the "low Kansas" of "Andy" Richards. "But Bristow," wrote White, "can and does talk the Kansas language, pure and undefiled, with the bark on; hot, turbulent and impassioned." There were times when Bristow spoke as if using a megaphone: The people understood what he was saying, but did not see the man behind the voice.[21] The article showed clearly the difference between the two men and emphasized that Bristow was closer to the needs of the people of Kansas than Long. Long was suave and polished and had platform finesse, but Bristow was tall and ungainly, and often his voice was not pleasing to his listeners. White's sharpest barb at Long came in "The Strange Case for Senator Long," in which White declared that if any ideas of progress could be "bored into his brain" he would make the best senator in the United States.[22] White stressed Bristow's courageous record as a public servant and the hard row "Joe" had faced in his early years. Through Senator LaFollette, but at his own expense, White had secured Long's voting record in Washington, tabulating 690 votes. Long felt that he needed to explain only thirty-five of the total votes, and he hurt his cause when he met

White on the speakers' platform in Emporia and derided White's accusations. When Long invited Senator Dolliver to come to Kansas to defend Long's record, White brought Senator LaFollette to tour the state for Bristow, announcing that when LaFollette "tells the people [that Long's record] is the worst he has ever examined in all his career it means something. . . . It means he knows and trusts Bristow." LaFollette used the record of roll-call votes in a devastating manner against Long.[23] White continued his search for financial aid, and when the campaign lagged he criticized Bristow for not putting enough life into his endeavor. And, finally, it was White who persuaded Norman Hapgood to publish in *Collier's Weekly* articles that linked Long with Aldrich and branded the incumbent senator as one of the undesirables.[24]

Midway in the campaign the supporters of both men began to agitate for a public debate between Long and Bristow. Bristow answered Long's Emporia speech at a banquet arranged by the Wichita Chamber of Commerce; he criticized Long's position on the long- and short-haul controversy, and his mastery of the railroad problems seemed to be winning him exceptional support.[25] It was agreed that Bristow would debate Long from the Sterling Chautauqua platform on July 14. Long was the polished speaker, but Bristow proved himself to be a shrewd antagonist. At Sterling, Bristow hit hard at the railroad abuses and asked five questions intended to prove Long's defection in the Senate. Long refused to answer Bristow's questions. Instead he delivered a low blow at Bristow by reading the letter Bristow had written to him in 1905 seeking the Panama appointment and criticizing President Roosevelt. The Emporia *Gazette* made much of Long's failure to answer Bristow. One headline ran, "Forty-Eight Hours and No Answer," and a later one, "Ninety-Six Hours and No Answer."[26] In a poem entitled "Chester's Silence," Walt Mason, the syndicated newspaper poet of terse verse, dramatized Long's refusal to answer:

> *But he will not answer questions*
> *And he won't tell where he's at.*

He is pointing at his record
And his record's pointing back,
And it oft flies up and hits him
With a solar plexus whack.[27]

Long and Bristow met on the speakers' platform in Topeka during the last week of the primary contest. There a noisy crowd demanded that Long answer Bristow. Bristow asked Long if he believed in a law for publicizing campaign contributions. Long replied that he did and then sprung a statement supposedly certified by a county clerk showing that Bristow had evaded the Kansas publicity law when he was secretary of the Republican state committee. Bristow replied that Long's backer, "Cy" Leland, knew more about where the money had come from. Long again read the 1905 letter and accused Bristow of being more like LaFollette than Theodore Roosevelt. Bristow did not deny the accusation.[28] Long was "fearfully puffed up," Bristow wrote later, and realized that he was defeated in the "last debate in Topeka."[29]

Three midwestern states, Kansas, Missouri, and Oklahoma, held primary elections on August 4, 1908. The Topeka *Capital* predicted a Bristow victory on election day, and as the returns began to come in, it was clear that Bristow was in the lead. By noon of August 5, the outlook was even brighter when thirty-four counties in western Kansas wired in victories for Bristow. At 2:30 in the afternoon, Morton Albaugh conceded Bristow's victory with the terse comment, "There is nothing to be said about it, it has been a hard fight and we had confidently hoped to win, but it is plainly evident that we lost."[30] By then Bristow had carried 89 of 165 senatorial and representative districts and was leading Long by over 35,000 popular votes. On August 6, Bristow thanked the Republicans for his nomination, stating that he had made the campaign in behalf of measures he "thought right." He declared that he was "dedicated to Roosevelt's policies" and that he stood in "confidential relation" with Taft.[31]

The primary gave a clear victory to Bristow. His following

was strongest in the western section of the state, where he had worked so diligently for irrigation in the 1890's. He had campaigned for fifteen weeks, often traveling with a borrowed horse and buggy, speaking in city halls rented by his friends. According to his own record, he had visited eighty counties and had made nearly one hundred speeches.[32] The campaign had been conducted in an atmosphere charged with anti-railroad and anti-corporation sentiment, and Bristow had emphasized his anti-railroad position with success. Long felt that he had been defeated, in part, by Democrats and Independents, non-Republicans who called for Republican ballots at the polls.[33] But editorial opinion on the whole agreed that Long had become too closely identified with the ruling clique in the Senate and had lost his standing with the people in Kansas. At the state level the Republicans were seeking freedom from the shackles of boss rule, and it was easy to look upon Long as one who was chronically and constitutionally opposed to the progressive movement in all its phases. The primary law had restored the political power of the people, and they had made the most natural use of it in the senatorial contest.[34]

Congratulatory messages came from supporters all over the United States. By August 8, Bristow had received some one hundred telegrams and over one thousand letters, and by August 31 the congratulatory messages numbered over three thousand.[35] President L. H. Murlin of Baker University congratulated Bristow on the "high and manly" manner in which he had conducted the campaign. "Every effort," wrote Murlin, "was made to throw dust in the eyes of the people by your opponents and thus blind them to the national issues, but you kept out of the side issues and held strictly to principles and convictions."[36] William A. Johnston, chief justice of the Kansas Supreme Court, wrote, "You were candid and direct, he [Long] was artfully clouding the issue and trying to get in on Taft's record instead of his own." Johnston recognized the value of the work of White and others but gave Bristow most of the credit for the victory. According to Johnston, it was the "clash between Long and yourself and the way you met the issues" that won the fight.[37] Bristow described the campaign to P. V. DeGraw, fourth assistant postmaster-general, as a hard fight against a strong enemy, well entrenched in official position and supplied with almost unlimited resources. "But," wrote Joe, "I had the people with me."[38] To Harold T. Chase, Bristow wrote, "I won solely because I was standing for things the people believed in and they believed I was sincere in advocating these things."[39] The impact of the primary law was fully acknowledged by Bristow in a letter to Judge Ben Lindsey when he declared he had won because the people had "the right to express their choice."[40] On December 5, 1908, he wrote to John E. Benton of New Hampshire, who was working for the primary election in his state, that not one in ten Kansans would vote to repeal the primary law.[41]

There were lighter moments in Bristow's victory. On August 11 he wrote to Bishop William Quayle, his former classmate, "Now is it not interesting that you should be made a bishop and I nominated for the United States Senate during the same year?" He confided to his friend that the conditions were fine for a "fall victory" and that his "great battle" was over. To another college friend, Samuel McRoberts, Bristow wrote, "When Quinn [Quayle's nickname] was made a Bishop, I felt like I wanted to win the Senatorship in Kansas, because I did not want the preachers to outclass us laymen in the race of life."[42]

On the day that Bristow was nominated, Senator William B. Allison of Iowa died. It was apparent that Governor Albert B. Cummins would be his successor as the Republican candidate for the Senate. In a sense Cummins represented all that Bristow stood for in Kansas. Cummins had the support of many Republicans in his state, but he was not in harmony with the old-guard supporters of Senator Jonathan Dolliver. Cummins was described by one of his supporters as follows: "He is a man of great ability, high personal character, aggressive, forceful and has largely the qualities of personal leadership as shown by the following he has built up in the State."[43] If the fall elections could be won by the Republicans, Cummins and Bristow would join Beveridge, Borah, and LaFollette in their Senate campaign against "Aldrichism."

On August 6, 1908, William Allen White wrote to Cummins, "We have just won Kansas from the machine by about 25,000, probably more and have nominated J. L. Bristow for the Senate over Chester I. Long, who by the way had the support of Senator Dolliver." White described his own connections with leading periodicals and newspapers and offered to write an article on Cummins' work and aims, "if it would help." White declared, "I feel a real desire to serve my country by helping such men as you. There is no office under the government that I would take."[44]

The local impact of Bristow's nomination was colorfully described by Cora Wellhouse Bullard, an amateur horticulturist and literary figure in Tonganoxie, Kansas. On August 24, 1908, Mrs. Bullard wrote to Senator Dolliver that she was sorry that Long would not go back to Washington. "I have been wondering," wrote Mrs. Bullard, "if we Kansans are not too much given to emotional theories and subjective judgments. However, in the defeat of Mr. Long, we have rendered William Allen White, our pet and hero, supremely happy, and that ought to be sufficient for us. Mr. Bristow's nomination being equivalent to an election, you will therefore have a new 'radical' in your ranks. Perhaps this may not be so bad for Kansas after all." Mrs. Bullard closed her letter with a somewhat flowery evaluation of the primary election:

> Generally speaking, we are greatly pleased with the first trial of our new primary law. Reading between the lines of the big print events, there seems to be a wonderous drawing of new powers all over the land. And in Kansas demagogic despotism is westering—falling towards eventide without a bit of doubt. I am sufficiently optimistic to believe that through the "direct primary" a mighty ministry shall be wrought up into the proportion and music of things. And into the policy of statesmanship there shall enter a nobler spirit, the spirit of rectitude and honesty, equity and patriotism. With the direct primary vote, the political boss must come with penitential voice—with humiliation, restitution and amendment. And he will

pray to be taken into co-operation with honest folks. Am I not right?[45]

The Democrats had nominated Hugh P. Farrelly from Chanute, Kansas, as Bristow's opponent. Farrelly had served in the state legislature from Neosho County and had been a candidate for other state offices. He had taken a leading part in the Democrat-Populist fusion in 1900. Farrelly could defeat Bristow only by securing a legislature with Democrats in the majority, normally a difficult task in Kansas.

There was some discontent among the Republicans. Some doubted that Taft would live up to Roosevelt's record; as White suggested, Taft might take a notion to let the Senate be "filthy still."[46] Rumors went around that the railroad interests were working for a Democratic victory. Bristow wrote Congressman Philip P. Campbell on August 11, 1908, "We will have a fight in Kansas because the 'interests' would rather see the state go to Bryan and Hugh Farrelly than to have Taft carry it and me elected."[47] Campbell replied assuring Bristow that some of the "warmest supporters" of Senator Long were now Bristow's "ardent supporters." He urged Joe to prepare the best Republican speech "you have ever made in your life" and deliver it in every county of the state. "Make it warm," wrote Campbell, and he pointed out that there was some fear among the "boys" that Bristow would not make a speech that would attract the old-line Republicans.[48]

The Republicans prepared for a hard campaign. Harold T. Chase drafted the Republican platform, which White declared was "too much endorsement" and "not enough recommendation." White felt that the party should press for railroad legislation in Kansas similar to that in Wisconsin or Michigan.[49] On August 16 the Topeka *Capital* published a full account of Bristow's life. Pictures of the family and of the Salina home and newspaper office were printed. The *Journal's* office was called the "neatest little newspaper office and print shop in the state," and Bristow was described as a man who was "never satisfied unless he was doing something in the public service." Joseph N. Dolley, chairman of the Republican state committee, invited many national leaders to campaign in Kansas. Beveridge, Borah, Cummins, Cannon, and LaFollette were among those who accepted the invitations.

Bristow engaged in a strenuous campaign and to some extent carried weak Republicans on his shoulders to the state legislature. Bristow's father wrote that at Baldwin party men worked hard to keep Republicans in line for John L. Brady. He believed that many would not have voted for him if Bristow's election had not depended on it. He also claimed that "we were able" to get several Democrats to "skip over" and support Republicans.[50] Bristow kept close contacts with the critical counties and stirred up local support with charges of corporate opposition. He opposed Bryan's stand on a national bank guarantee law and wrote an article for the Kansas City *Star* in which he stated that he was afraid that Kansas banks would have to pay for others' losses. His speaking schedule was crowded: between October 20 and October 31 he spoke in eighteen towns. Toward the end of the campaign, after giving 140 speeches in five and one-half months, he wrote to Capper that he was very tired.[51]

But his work was well rewarded. On November 7 he reported that on the joint legislative ballot were 123 Republicans and 42 Democrats. Bristow would have a majority on the legislative ballot for senator.[52] Walt Mason of the Emporia *Gazette* congratulated Bristow: "You have made a wonderful campaign, and those who were inclined to scoff at the beginning finally remained to pray and vote for you. Kansas people are expecting great things of you."[53] On November 9, President-elect Taft sent his congratulations to Bristow. Bristow wrote on November 14 that Bryan's question, "Shall the people rule?" had been answered. According to Bristow, "the people always did rule and always will. The question is how shall they rule and what policies will they decide upon. In the late election they decided in favor of progressive conservatives."[54]

The weeks following the election were busy ones for Bristow. There were many business matters to arrange and scores of letters to answer. Through his press associates he sought recommendations for an editor for the *Evening Journal*. The *Journal* at the time was grossing $36,000 a year with daily advertising running over $1,000 a month.[55] Late in November it was announced that Paul Lovewell, an experienced editor and a hard worker, had been hired. At the same time Cecil Howes, Topeka correspondent for the Kansas City *Star,* applied for the job as Topeka correspondent to the *Journal*.[56] Bristow's second son, Frank, became business manager of the Salina publication. The Bristow family planned to remain in Salina for the first session of Congress.

Bristow's correspondence shows that he was seeking advice from political leaders on the issues he would face in Washington, and his local associates pressed him to assist the newly elected governor, Stubbs, with the state legislative program.[57] There were the usual requests from office seekers.[58] In December a rumor spread that President-elect Taft might select Senator Long for a cabinet post. Bristow wrote a sharp protest to Taft, insisting that Kansas Republicans would not support such an appointment. During the same month he counseled Taft not to interfere in the contest in the House of Representatives over the speakership, but to insist that certain pledges that the party had made be carried through.[59]

Bristow corresponded with Cummins, and from Senator Dolliver he sought advice about a lyceum company with which he might become associated. Dolliver recommended the Central Lyceum Bureau of Kansas City, directed by A. E. Palmer, and he urged Bristow to "give some time to lecture work. It does a man no harm and gives him the opportunity not only to do good, but also to make a little money—a very important item in a world like this."[60] Bristow followed Dolliver's advice, and by 1910 he was regarded as a very effective Chautauqua speaker.

On January 27, 1909, the Kansas legislature met to select a United States senator. This was the first time the legislators had gathered in separate session to elect a senator after the people had already instructed them how to vote. Representative A. C. Mitchell, a Republican from Douglas County, nominated Bristow, and Representative T. F. Morrison, a Democrat from Neosho County, nominated Hugh P. Farrelly. The legislators voted as instructed. All Republicans, plus one Independent, voted for Bristow, and the Democrats voted for Farrelly. Bristow's total was 115 to Farrelly's 46. On the next day, in a formal ceremony, Bristow was presented with his official notice of election. His family and many friends were present. In his acceptance address Bristow once again struck out at railway abuses. He reviewed the famous Chicago and Alton Railway case and declared that Gould and Harrison, like bank robbers, should face imprisonment for their crimes. He referred to his own work with the Panama Canal and pledged to aid in tariff revision, and he urged all Kansans to assist him with advice and counsel.[61] The new senator appeared to be impressed by the political responsibilities that he was soon to face in Washington.

6

Early Months in Washington

Inaugural ceremonies in Washington are usually impressive, and during inaugural week many lasting impressions are made upon the new members who enter Congress, as well as upon the old members who take careful measure of the new arrivals. Skilled representatives of the press try to measure the political strength and predict the futures of the new arrivals for their readers.

In 1909 political observers knew that the changing of the political guard was significant and charged with tension. The electors in 1908 had sent representatives of the liberal wing in both parties to Congress, but they had also chosen a President who, from the first flush of victory, appeared to be moving away from the insurgent element of his own party.[1] Of the ninety senators who had been in Congress when President Theodore Roosevelt took his oath of office in 1905, only thirty-five returned in 1909. Twenty-nine new senators took the oath in March, 1909; twelve were new men in Congress. Joseph L. Bristow was one of the new arrivals who had won his place in the liberal wing of his party. The political editor of the Washington *Post* wrote long descriptions of the new senators. He wrote that Bristow "ought to be an insurgent, for his has been a most strenuous career."[2] The editor described Bristow's work as fourth assistant postmaster-general and predicted that congressmen would not soon forget the Bristow report and the charges Bristow had brought against certain members of the House. Nor would Bristow's courageous investigations, which resulted in sending more men to the penitentiary within a given period than ever before in the history of the government, be forgotten. The editor, while placing Bristow on the liberal side, predicted that the liberals' path would not be strewn with roses.

Bristow was deeply indebted to the liberal side of his party when he arrived in Washington. For years he had been carefully assessing the strength of his own political beliefs. To Bristow politics was a science of performance rather than a technique of posturing. And he knew that from the homes of the midwestern United States demands were being made for legislative bodies to consider human welfare. Successful politics in 1909 had to be directed along the lines of public service.

From the time of his victory in the primaries, Bristow had been looking for an issue that he might support when he entered the Senate. William Allen White had pressed him to sound the alarm against the evils in interstate transportation, and Bristow had responded to this when he spoke to the state legislature in January, but he was not certain that this would be the issue to pursue in the future. He watched the maneuvers of the newly elected President. He, like other liberals, wanted President Taft on his side. Seen from Kansas, Taft seemed to be moving to the side of the conservatives. On February 4, 1909, Bristow wrote to his old friend J. R. Harrison that if Taft deserted the liberals he would "annihilate himself." Such a weakening would not hurt LaFollette, Cummins, and the rest "if we stand up and fight, and I am going to fight whether they do or not."[3] This letter made clear the fact that Bristow considered himself in the company of the outstanding liberals from the Midwest.

Bristow, although he had lived in Washington before, was

stimulated by his new position and surroundings, and he vividly reported his reactions in various letters to the folks back home. He described the inaugural ceremonies to his son Frank: March 4, 1909, was "the worst day Washington has had all winter, so they say." There were six to eight inches of slushy snow on the ground and a strong northwest wind; "nevertheless the crowds were large and disorderly." Senator Charles Curtis escorted Bristow to the rostrum, where he was sworn in. To Bristow the ceremony was impressive, but not as impressive as the joint session of the Kansas legislature, "because there were too many fellows in the crowd yesterday . . . the President and Vice-President and thirty new Senators, while in Kansas I was the only fellow in it." "But after all," he wrote, "this was the real thing, and to use the Kansas phrase, it put me on the payroll, which seems to be the uppermost thought in the minds of the average Kansan."[4]

On March 10, Bristow talked with President Taft on patronage matters. Taft assured Bristow that he would recognize the senators' interests in appointments to state-wide offices and that he would reserve the post offices for congressmen. This had been the policy of Taft's predecessors for some time. Taft did not want to remove persons from office except for official reasons, but at the expiration of the regular term of office he would consider the office vacant.[5]

Through his letters to Frank Bristow and to Harold T. Chase of Topeka, Bristow recorded his early evaluations of his new congressional associates. He found a real interest in the organization of the House. There Augustus P. (Gussie) Gardner, the son-in-law of Henry Cabot Lodge, was leading the insurgents, and "Gussie" was against Lodge as often as for him. Victor Murdock, according to Bristow, got more advertising out of his work, but the "real hero" of the Kansas delegation was "Ed" Madison. His associates felt that Madison was "not much of a grandstander" and "was more dependable in critical times." Bristow was "very much taken" with Senator Albert B. Cummins of Iowa and found him to be the most attractive member of the "new crowd" he had met. He described Cummins as a man of unusual strength, possessing striking elements of leadership, thoroughly aggressive and systematic in his work, very intelligent, and well informed, as well as a courageous and persistent fighter. Cummins had a pleasing personality and mingled with the senators in a cordial way. Because of his friendliness, Bristow predicted that Cummins would be more successful in managing a fight in the Senate than Robert M. LaFollette, but would never impress the country "as LaFollette has."[6]

Bristow regarded LaFollette as "the ablest of all the progressives." He was the crusader, the pioneer, who had blazed the way and opened the road for the "rest of us to follow him." In doing so LaFollette had incurred the personal and relentless hostility of "men who believed in things that *are*." "They devote their hatred and resentment to him far more than they do to the rest of us who have followed on the path that he has marked out." The conservative Senator Nelson A. Aldrich and his crowd had no use for Bristow, but they were not "so violently prejudiced" against Cummins and Bristow as they were against LaFollette. Aldrich and his friends despised LaFollette and, in Bristow's words, took "personal pleasure in handicapping him in every way they can." Bristow described LaFollette as a "peculiar man" in some respects. He was a very sensitive man, who "keenly felt a discourtesy or snub of any kind." He did not mingle freely with the other senators and spent a great deal of his time in his committee room studying and investigating the subjects in which he was interested. This did not give him the personal relationships that were so influential in legislative bodies. Few senators knew him in a personal way. Yet, in spite of his seclusive habits, he was among the "ablest and best informed" of any of the senators on the things in which he was interested. On the floor of the Senate, according to Bristow, "Aldrich could not be compared to LaFollette."[7]

Bristow struck up an early friendship with Senator Henry A. du Pont. "Old man duPont of Delaware, a rich aristrocrat, and I are becoming close friends," he wrote. "He is a liberal minded old fellow and honest, but of course his opinions are influenced very

Cartoon from Kansas City *Journal,* July 10, 1910

"The Big Boss Aroused at Last,"
Topeka *State Journal,* August 11, 1910

Senator Bristow, June 13, 1900
Kansas State Historical Society

Mrs. Joseph L. Bristow,
about 1906

much by his environment. Yet he is a pretty broad minded old fellow and is very fair and considerate." Bristow described Norris Brown of Nebraska as an "aggressive, forcible fighter for the right things." He felt that Elmer Burkett of Nebraska trailed along about the same as Curtis "does in Kansas." During the first weeks in Congress, Bristow was treated well by Curtis. However, he described his senior associate as being with the progressives "in all things that are not vital" and predicted he "may be with us on some vital things." But Bristow knew that Curtis had no spirit of the martyr in his heart. Coe Crawford of South Dakota was aggressively on the right side, but Bristow was not too certain as to the strength of Martin N. Johnson of North Dakota and Wesley L. Jones of Washington. Both had been elected under the progressive banner. In his evaluation of his associates in the Senate, Bristow underestimated the political strength of Jonathan P. Dolliver and Albert J. Beveridge. He described Beveridge as "pretty good" and Dolliver as "fair." After working shoulder to shoulder with these two colleagues in the fight over tariff revision, Bristow found them both to be skilled and powerful parliamentarians.[8]

Bristow's first impressions of his associates, on the whole, stood the test of time. Although he may have erred in judgment concerning the political strength of some individuals, he keenly sensed the political atmosphere in which the liberals had to work during the special session of Congress.

While measuring and evaluating his associates, Bristow was also looking for able and influential Kansans he might recommend for appointment. Early in Taft's administration it was learned that the Secretary of Agriculture, James Wilson, would not remain in office. Bristow tried to interest Arthur Capper in becoming Wilson's successor, stressing "that Capper was the only man in the state . . . to push for the place." Capper pleaded lack of experience. Defending his recommendation, Bristow replied that the current Secretary of Treasury, Franklin MacVeagh, "never held office in his life." He had been in the wholesale grocery business. Bristow wanted a man with "good practical business sense" as head of the Department of Agriculture. Referring to the recent appointment of their friend Quayle as a Methodist bishop, Bristow bantered Capper: "I would really rather risk you as a member of the cabinet than as a Methodist bishop. I think you would fit the job better. I wouldn't recommend you for a Methodist bishop, but I would be glad to exert all the influence that I may be able to accumulate to get you in the cabinet."[9] The young Kansas editor did not press for the appointment. Meanwhile, Bristow was busy selecting an office staff, working for Senate committees, and expanding his investments in Salina, Kansas.

Bristow was given a large suite on the third floor of the new Senate office building, by chance near Senators Aldrich, Hale, Cullom, and other conservatives.[10] Two young Kansans joined his staff. His search for a "good clean newspaper man" ended when Cleo C. Hardy of Ottawa accepted the publicity assignment at a salary of $1,400.[11] In April, Bristow hired Fay N. Seaton as his private secretary. Seaton was born and raised in Jewell County. As a young man he loved newspaper work and often hung around the Salina *Journal* office while he was attending Kansas Wesleyan University. He worked a few months with the Chicago Civic League and then became a private secretary to one of the public utility commissioners appointed by Governor Charles Evans Hughes of New York. Bristow felt that although Seaton was not trained in politics, it would not take him long to learn. During his one and one-half years in New York, Seaton had joined three political clubs, backed a winner to Congress, and attended the Taft inaugural ceremonies. He left a $2,200 position for a $2,220 one with Bristow.[12] Hardy and Seaton remained in Washington while Bristow was in the Senate. Both men entered the newspaper business in Kansas when Bristow was defeated in 1914. Seaton purchased the Manhattan *Mercury-Chronicle* and was the founder of the present-day Seaton chain of newspapers.

In February, Bristow negotiated the purchase of a forty-eight-acre tract of land in the southeast part of Salina for $9,450. He had a good sense of real estate values, especially real estate that would increase in value because of its strategic importance. He had purchased the Gilbert School tract next to his home at 435 Santa Fe Street in 1905. In borrowing the money for that purchase, he assured his banker that the Salina *Journal* was "carrying itself" and that he would pay off the mortgage for the new land from his earnings in Washington.[13]

Like all new senators Bristow worried over his committee assignments. On March 15 he wrote to Senator Aldrich, the chairman of the committees, stating his preference as follows: (1) Interstate Commerce, (2) Commerce, (3) Interoceanic Canals, (4) Post Office and Post Roads.[14] He confided to C. B. Kirtland that Senators LaFollette and Cummins were not getting their desires and that he would not get Commerce or Postal, "but important ones where I will be properly recognized and do no harm."[15] Only four days later he wrote to Governor Stubbs in Kansas that the progressives had gotten on every committee and, according to LaFollette and Cummins, "had a much better vantage ground" than ever before.[16] Bristow's first committee assignments included Claims Committee, Interoceanic Canals, Railroads, Transportation Routes to the Seaboard, and the Committee on Standards, Weights, and Measures. In the next session of Congress, he became chairman of the Committee on Expenditures in the Post Office Department and was given other assignments, on the Claims Committee and on the Committee on Public Health and National Quarantine.[17]

If Senator Bristow believed that he could pursue a leisurely pace in the Senate and select his own issues with care, he was badly mistaken. One month after his arrival in Washington he became an active participant in one of the greatest tariff debates in the nation's history; a debate that not only left lasting impressions on the new senator but also aligned him on a liberal course for the next six years.

For seven years President Theodore Roosevelt had skillfully delayed a showdown in Congress on tariff revision. At the beginning of his campaign, William Howard Taft had promised tariff revision, and after the election he had backed away from a party struggle over the selection of Joseph Cannon as Speaker of the

House in order to secure the support of the conservative Republicans for tariff reform. Taft called a special session of Congress for March, 1909, to modify the Dingley tariff rates. Sereno E. Payne guided the new tariff proposal in the House, where it met little difficulty. It was not all that the revisionists desired, but it contained substantial reductions for many rates. The Aldrich bill introduced in the Senate on April 12, however, contained over eight hundred amendments to the House bill, most of them sending the rates back up again. Shocked at this defeat for President Taft, the liberal newspaper editors of the Midwest urged their senators and representatives to join Taft and defeat the powerful eastern cabal headed by Senator Aldrich.[18]

Bristow was not well informed on the tariff rates and he made no claim to be so. He believed that the tariff had been used to foster monopolies, and he had supported his party's promise for revision. Like most midwestern progressives he was not a free trader, but he argued that the nation had followed a shortsighted policy that had hastened the exploitation of the great resources so essential to its own welfare. He also stressed the need for a system of maximum and minimum rates under which the President would be given authority to adjust tariffs to promote the business interests of the country. In private conversations with the President he became convinced that Taft wanted genuine downward revision, and he felt sure that the Senate revisions were not in the public interest.[19] Like others from the Midwest he was aghast at the Aldrich proposals. He aligned himself quickly with Senators LaFollette, Cummins, Dolliver, Clapp, and Beveridge, who made up the hard core of progressive opposition to high tariff.

Unprepared, Bristow first entered the debate against the high rates on lead and zinc. He insisted that he would uphold his position unless all kinds of leather goods were placed on the free list. At the same time he demanded free lumber, coal, iron, and pig iron so that a little town in Kansas could run a foundry with no danger of a big steel company's cornering the raw materials.[20] In the early discussions he got trounced. He admitted to his son, "I didn't know anything about the lead business, but circumstances threw me into the controversy, and I had to learn about it."[21] Furthermore, "speaking to the United States Senate was a much different proposition from talking in country school houses out on the prairies."[22]

This first encounter proved to Bristow that the opponents of high rates must first of all be informed. "To become familiar with the tariff," he wrote, "is a work of a life time."[23] Each opponent to the Aldrich bill selected a special area of rates to study. Bristow's contact with commercial interests at the time he made the Panama study proved to be extremely valuable. He wrote to importers, old friends in the New York Customs House and the Port Authority in New York, and to Secretary of the Treasury MacVeagh. He was well reinforced with an extensive tariff bibliography from the Library of Congress.

Many of his former associates responded to his inquiries. Secretary MacVeagh furnished much information on the sugar rates. Some of the experts placed the Aldrich rates slightly higher than the Dingley rates. Senator Beveridge's findings showed a similar trend. Senator Dolliver's extensive correspondence with manufacturers clearly pointed out that the Aldrich forces had completely ignored the great savings to industry that had become possible through new manufacturing techniques and labor-saving machines. With the new manufacturing processes tariffs were no longer a necessity.[24]

Bristow was spurred to work harder than ever before. He complained that he "could not find hours enough in the day or sufficient physical strength to grasp and comprehend the innumerable and intricate details of the bill."[25] To Frank Bristow, who was raising poultry, he wrote, "I believe I would rather take care of the chickens than to try to make a tariff, although the tariff discussion is going to be intensely interesting."[26] Bristow's determination to study and present a clear-cut case was increased when Curtis, the senior senator from Kansas, urged Joe to get on the high-tariff side. Bristow soon learned, too, that many of his constituents in Kansas, like Curtis, did not want him on the low-tariff side. Shortly after his first debate he was flooded with protests from the oil, cattle, and zinc interests of the state. He assured his correspondents that they would not be injured by tariff reductions, although he saw more clearly than ever before that his future actions would be guided by the broad public interest of his constituents.

On May 6, in the midst of cries of "vote," he defied the old guard and insisted on his right to speak. Here the investigator of old, who never left the trail of a crooked deal until he reached the end of it, hunted down the smelter trust. The Washington correspondent for the Philadelphia *American* reported that Bristow was the "sensation" of the tariff fight and brought out even better than Dolliver the unreasonable rates of the proposed bill.[27] The fight in May was severe. Bristow held a three-day running debate on schedules, and his description of the affair was, "We got licked on every roll call and every vote, but still that doesn't discourage us."[28] During the debate Lodge had ridiculed LaFollette's stand on the tariff. LaFollette's reply was described by Bristow as the "severest thing" he had ever seen. "It was terrific.... I never saw a little fellow so charged with electric force and power."[29] Bristow described Dolliver's tariff speech as the "greatest speech I have ever heard."[30] But when the opposition was at its greatest there were only twelve to fourteen progressive supporters, and frequently support by the Democrats collapsed, with more supporting Aldrich than opposing him.[31]

The Aldrich supporters used every trick in the bag to deride Bristow and his fellow progressives. On May 22, Bristow wrote to Harold Chase, "When I arise, or other liberals do, I am treated with sneers and insulting remarks from the Aldrich coterie." He declared that there was "never a machine convention in its worst days in Kansas more intolerant ... discourteous and insulting every step of the way."[32] In the heat of the tariff debate, Bristow wrote to White that the tariff was being revised "by a band of legislative pirates, and we need some good magazine writers to help." He pointed out that the conservatives from the Rocky Mountain states, the Pacific coast, New York, Pennsylvania, West Virginia, and Louisiana controlled the Senate, and declared that from senators representing states west of Kansas, Nebraska, and South Dakota the progressive cause did not get a single vote, except that of Newlands from Nevada.[33]

While Bristow gathered information on many tariff schedules, he selected the sugar issue for his most thorough study. The United States was using the Dutch standard, an obsolete color test, to grade unrefined sugar. Through the use of the color test, much of the imported raw sugar was graded so low that it had to pass through American refineries before reaching the consumer. Meanwhile, the lighter, higher-quality brown sugar was assigned higher rates so that its use by the consumer was not economical. The lighter sugars, very valuable to the housewife in the canning season, were often unobtainable. Bristow's study showed that 110 out of 117 nations had discarded the Dutch standard and were using a polariscopic test which measured the actual saccharin purity of sugar. The Dutch standard had become simply a device that enabled the sugar trust to regulate the price paid to the producer of raw sugar, as well as the price of refined sugar paid by the consumer. Bristow described the Dutch standard as the "most infamous thing that was ever put in a tariff bill,"[34] but it took three sessions of Congress before Bristow defeated its use.

Bristow won the respect of many of his fellow senators by his able presentation of the sugar problem, and he could proudly record that he had had the gratifying experience of receiving the attention of every man in the Senate chamber when he spoke. This was because he was telling a story in regard to the sugar business "that was new and original."[35] Even President Taft invited Bristow to the White House for a briefing on the sugar schedule, and he did not try to interfere with the stand Bristow had taken.[36] Bristow felt that outwardly the President appeared to be moving to the support of the Aldrich crowd, but that "at heart" Taft was with the progressives.[37]

Throughout the tariff debate the midwestern senators avoided a direct public attack on Taft, although they hammered away constantly at Aldrich and Cannon as the symbols of vested interests. Taft, however, was either unwilling to use the tactics and tools of executive pressure or unconvinced by the liberals, and he threw his support in the closing hours of the struggle to the Aldrich crowd, leaving the progressive wing of his party isolated. Taft's ultimate defense of his position was that he had a legislative program to carry out and that he could not lose the support of the conservative wing of his party over tariff reform and still save the rest of his program. Actually he had reached this position early in the tariff debate, and the progressives were furnished ample evidence for their distrust of Taft.[38]

In the search for new sources of revenue, both the income tax and the corporation tax were proposed during the tariff debate. Several liberal Republicans backed the income tax. Conferences with President Taft led them to believe that Taft would be glad to see an income tax measure adopted. In fact he encouraged Borah and Cummins to go ahead and draft such a proposal.[39] Bristow spent many hours with Cummins in drafting the income tax measure. But once it was introduced, Taft began to give stronger support to the corporation tax. Taft believed that the question of the constitutionality of the income tax would again be placed before the Supreme Court, and that it was unlikely the Court would depart from precedents established in President Cleveland's second administration. The corporation tax would provide the nation with a quicker and an uncontested source of revenue. Bristow and his associates hoped the new income tax proposal might secure a reversal of the Supreme Court's past opinion. Gradually the President "picked off" the supporters of the income tax, and the Senate sustained the corporation tax.[40]

Bristow was sincere in his opposition to the corporation tax. He argued that the corporation tax did not apply with equal fairness to all money-making firms. Incorporated businesses had to pay the tax while partnerships and firms owned by a single person or family remained untaxed. He felt that the tax was merely an indirect tax on the consumer. He also stressed that the holders of profitable bonds were not reached by the corporation tax.[41] Throughout Taft's administration Bristow was an ardent supporter of the income tax, and in February, 1913, it became part of the Constitution, as the sixteenth amendment.

When the Payne-Aldrich bill emerged from the conference committee, it was still a high tariff proposal with most of the advantages assigned to the manufacturers in the East at the expense of the producers of raw materials of the West. Bristow and six of his Republican associates in the Senate, along with twenty Republicans in the House, voted against the final bill. The opponents openly declared that the bill did not live up to the party's campaign promises and threw most of the blame upon Aldrich and his followers. Throughout the Midwest leading Republican newspapers condemned the Payne-Aldrich proposal and called for the overthrow of the conservative leadership of the party. Outraged by four months of liberal opposition, the President widened the break with the liberals by his own actions and kindled the flames of the progressive revolt which was to follow. Taft upheld the Payne-Aldrich tariff as the best ever passed. He struck out at the "muckraking" press. He gave special thanks to the conservative Senator Charles Curtis from Kansas for his help and willingness to take the denunciation of the newspapers at home in order to "ease the course" of the administration. He slighted liberals by not inviting them to join the Presidential train as he toured the country in the autumn of 1909. According to Taft, they were no longer Republicans but "assistant Democrats."[42]

Bristow's response to the President's attitude did not differ from that of his liberal associates. In public he refrained from open criticism of President Taft, and in his private correspondence he cautioned his associates against an open break with the President. On September 20, 1909, he wrote to Senator Cummins that he was "surprised" at Taft's attitude; it looked as if Taft had completely "surrendered to Aldrich." The battle, wrote Bristow, that LaFollette and Cummins had started ten years ago "has just fairly begun." He saw no "prospect for rest" ahead; he planned to face the issue squarely in Kansas, "treating the President with respect" but fighting for a "genuine and honest revision."[43] The real issue, in Bristow's words, was whether the Republicans in the

Midwest "would accept the leadership of Aldrich, Hale, Cannon and Payne" or follow the views of the men who had acquired the name "which some people use to disparage them, but which I use with a good deal of pride—'Insurgents.' "[44]

The impact of the special session of Congress could not be thrown off lightly by the junior senator from Kansas. He had learned many lessons; some the hard way. He had withstood the vicious cartooning of the conservative press and the hostile taunts of the conservatives on the Senate floor. Once again he had demonstrated that he was a capable and well-informed opponent against the forces of corruption and entrenched conservatism.

The Maturing Senator

At the close of the special session of Congress in the summer of 1909, Senator Bristow returned to Salina, where there were many matters, personal, business, and political, to occupy his time. Before leaving Washington he had rented a house at 1300 Freemont Street, and he made plans to close the Salina home during the next congressional session. Winter temperatures in the capital were indicated in a letter to his oldest son, Joseph Q., asking him to order seven tons of furnace coal, three tons of range coal, and a cord of wood for the winter.[1] His second son, Frank had decided to give up the management of the Salina *Journal* and return to law school. This was indeed a fortunate decision: in 1910 he was granted a Rhodes scholarship to study in Oxford.[2] Bristow wanted Joseph to give up his civil service position in Washington and return to Salina to manage the *Journal,* but "young Joe" elected to remain in Washington, where he could make more money and have "a great deal better time."[3] The youngest son, Ed, planned to enter Baker University in the fall; he would live with his grandfather at Baldwin.[4]

Bristow consulted several newspapermen in his search for a

business manager. His stand on prohibition was clearly shown when he wrote to a friend, Fred C. Trigg, "but I want a teetotaler. Anyone who drinks need not apply."[5] At the same time he sought advice from Henry Allen and Victor Murdock on the installation of a new accounting system for the office. C. F. Lebow became business manager; he was succeeded later by H. W. Moffat. The circulation of the *Journal* had reached nearly four thousand by the spring of 1910.[6] Bristow purchased Allen's half-share of the *Journal* building and made plans to add a second story.

During the fall of 1909, Bristow guided the *Journal* in civic controversies. He backed the movement for the city of Salina to acquire its own waterworks; the measure lost in the city election by 269 votes. Bristow opposed the renewal of a private franchise for electric lights because the franchise did not contain a clause granting the city the right to purchase the electric business, if the people should desire such a plan. He also supported the drive for the local YMCA building.[7]

Bristow and his staff compiled lists of Kansas voters during the congressional recess. Farm women, boys' and girls' clubs, women's clubs, and many other organizations were included, and by midsummer of 1910 he had the names of approximately sixty thousand Republicans and five thousand Democrats. He mailed out not only his own speeches, but also those of the fellow progressives—often in ten- to twenty-thousand lots. He wrote Robert P. Bass, insurgent candidate for the governorship of New Hampshire, that it was easier to interest the young men than the old in politics. He found the old soldiers and the young men most enthusiastic, "the old soldier because you could arouse in him a patriotism and the young man because he was full of ambition and progressive ideas."[8]

Throughout the fall of 1909, Bristow traveled in the state, sampling public opinion, defending his vote on the tariff, and attacking Aldrich and Cannon. He was highly pleased with his reception, and he confided to Senator Beveridge that President Taft's attitude would "not change 1000 votes" in Kansas.[9] Bristow's position on the tariff seemed to be vindicated by the results of a poll conducted by the editor of the farm publication *Mail and Breeze*. The question asked was: "Do you approve of the course of Senator Bristow in voting against the tariff bill that was passed at the special session of Congress?" The replies were:

	Yes	No
Republicans	632	45
Democrats	219	1
Socialists	48	1
Prohibitionists	25	1
Independents	139	1
Totals	1063	49[10]

During his tour of the state, Bristow used every opportunity to strike at Speaker Cannon, not only in the party's interest but also in the interest of good government. When Charles W. Scott of Iola, Kansas, criticized his attitude toward the Speaker, Bristow replied that he thought Cannon was "a menace to the welfare of the Republican Party" and an impediment in the road of all progressive legislation.[11] As for Aldrich and Taft, Bristow wrote on November 1 that if they did not change, every one of "these Western states would become overwhelmingly Democratic."[12] Meanwhile, the midwestern progressives were shaping the battle line for the coming session of Congress. On a trip down the Mississippi River with the Inland Waterways Commission, a group of progressives made plans to attack the conservative leadership in Congress. Few victories were anticipated, but it was hoped that the drive for liberal principles would lead to the election of a Congress which was "worth something" in November of 1910.[13]

On his return to Washington in December, 1909, Bristow met with the editors of *Collier's, Success,* and *McClure's* magazines to discuss publicity to be given to the efforts of the progressives. *McClure's* would feature articles on conservation, *Success* would fight Cannon, and *Collier's* would follow the same policy toward railroads that it had previously. Once again the progressives would stress particular issues: Bristow would make a drive for the

direct election of senators, Borah would press for postal savings banks, Cummins would lead the fight to strengthen the power of the Interstate Commerce Commission, while LaFollette and Beveridge planned to press for a tariff commission.[14]

The midwestern Republicans, while suspicious of an alliance between President Taft and the conservatives, tried not to get into a direct fight with the administration.[15]

The decision that the junior senator from Kansas would carry the workload for the direct election of senators undoubtedly led to one of Bristow's major contributions to American government. The idea of the selection of senators by direct vote was nearly a century old: it was first introduced into Congress in 1826. By 1909 approximately forty resolutions involving the idea had been introduced into Congress. Members of the House were more sympathetic toward adoption than were senators; in the Senate it was difficult to secure a favorable report from the Committee on Privileges and Elections, the committee to which the proposal was most frequently referred. During his first month in the Senate, Bristow had proposed the modification of Section 3 of the Constitution to allow for the direct election of senators by the people. He tied his proposal to Senator Cummins' income tax proposal; both failed at that time.[16] In the next congressional session Bristow turned to a direct amendment to the Constitution,[17] but as in his tariff fight over the Dutch standard, Bristow had to work persistently for three years before his amendment became the fundamental law of the land.

Friends encouraged Bristow to assign his proposal to the Judiciary Committee, where it might receive more favorable treatment. Once assigned, it was not reported out of the committee for nearly sixteen months, in spite of Bristow's use of every parliamentary device at his disposal. The proposed amendment called for national supervision of the election of senators on the same basis as in elections of members to the House of Representatives, and a bitter fight was led by southern Democrats over the right of the states to control the election of senators. After considerable maneuvering the progressives placed Senator Borah on a subcommittee of the Judiciary Committee. Through hard work Borah eventually got the Bristow resolution to the floor of the Senate, in February, 1911, but the resolution was defeated.[18]

Ten United States senators who had voted against the Bristow proposal in 1909 were retired in the election of 1910, and six newly elected senators favored the amendment. Bristow debated the issue in the spring of 1911. He was greatly encouraged in his fight when the Kansas legislature, in February, 1911, adopted a resolution urging its representatives and senators in Washington to support the proposal. Little that was new could be added to the debate, which had been current since Populist days. Bristow pointed out that thirty-three state legislatures had declared in favor, in substance if not in form, and four states had primary laws nominating senators by general election. He emphasized his great trust in the people's ability to select senators, in contrast with the views held in the early days of the Republic, maintaining that direct election would free the state legislatures from pressure and corruption and the country from greed and vested interests.[19]

Senator Borah secured a favorable report from the Judiciary Committee again on May 8, 1911, and on June 12, 1911, the Senate adopted the amendment by a vote of 64 to 24. Bristow wrote to White on May 14 that it was "exceedingly gratifying" to be the author of the first change in the fundamental law on representation since the early period of the Republic.[20] The New York *Tribune* praised Bristow's work, declaring that his opposition to state control of elections saved the entire proposition from defeat.[21] William Jennings Bryan and Champ Clark brought pressure on members of the House of Representatives, and the House accepted the proposal by a vote of 237 to 12 on May 13, 1912.

Bristow had done a signal job in keeping the issue before the Senate, but his task was not completed. State legislative approval had to follow. In February, 1913, Bristow shouldered the task of writing to all the secretaries of state and lieutenant governors to see if the proposed amendment was being considered. He was pleased when the name of his home state came in among the first twelve favorable responses. As each state fell into line, he sent new letters to those that had not acted. By February 21 twenty-three states had acted favorably; the number rose to thirty-one by March 13, 1913.[22] Bristow now called upon William Jennings Bryan, who had become United States Secretary of State, to exert pressure on his friends, especially in Delaware, New Jersey, Connecticut, and Rhode Island.[23] Connecticut was the thirty-third state to approve, and by April 9 thirty-six states had reported in favor. On that day Bristow wrote to Theodore Roosevelt that the seventeenth amendment was "now a part of the Constitution." He continued, "I think it is the most fundamental change in the Constitution that has been made and it is the first direct progressive achievement."[24]

Although, throughout the land newspapers supporting the issue credited the victory to the tireless and faithful work of Senators Bristow and Borah,[25] Bristow was not invited to the final ceremonies held by Bryan and President Wilson to amend the Constitution. Bryan brought in former Congressman Tucker of Virginia, a Democrat who had introduced a similar resolution twenty years before, and credited him with the accomplishment. The claim that this was a victory for the Democrats was a weak one, considering that only one Democrat in the Senate had voted for the amendment in the spring of 1911. Bristow was bitter over his failure to get recognition, but he did not speak out because he did not want to start a quarrel with the new administration.[26] Although the newly elected Democrats laid false claim to responsibility for the seventeenth amendment, the midwestern Republican leadership had won credit for the adoption of the sixteenth amendment, the income tax amendment, on February 25, 1913.[27]

Bristow made frequent use of the constitutional amending process to advance progressive principles and to "smoke out" the reactionary elements in Congress. In December, 1912, he introduced two resolutions to amend the Constitution. The first would allow the President to submit to the vote of the people measures on which Congress had refused to act. The second would allow the people to uphold by majority vote a congressional act which the Supreme Court had declared unconstitutional. There were

William L. Bristow,
Father of the Senator

Joseph Quayle Bristow,
Oldest Son of the Senator

Frank Baker Bristow,
Middle Son of the Senator

Edwin McKinley Bristow,
Youngest Son of the Senator

Ossian Hall, Home of Joseph L. Bristow
John O. Brostrop, Photographer; Library of Congress Collection

few chances that the ideas would be adopted, but they represented advanced progressivism. Theodore Roosevelt termed the proposals "admirable,"[28] and Gifford Pinchot called them "a great piece of work."[29] Bristow followed these with proposals for the election of postmasters by popular vote, for procedure for the recall of the President, and for woman suffrage. He became an ardent champion of woman suffrage, speaking on the subject more often than any other member of the Senate. The nineteenth amendment to the Constitution, adopted in the closing years of Wilson's administration, used the exact words of the amendment Bristow had introduced in 1913 and 1914.[30]

The amending process was not the only way in which Bristow sought to advance the tenets of progressivism. During the Taft administration Bristow took a stand on nearly every major political issue that came before the Senate, and he made it a rule to be present on the floor each day the Senate conducted business. Privately, Bristow expressed his belief that President Taft was out to destroy the insurgents, but he avoided public statements of his opinion.[31] His suspicions increased when he and Senator Curtis became locked in a bitter contest over patronage. Actually, Bristow and the President were closer in their views than either realized, but Taft interpreted the actions of Bristow and his fellow progressives as an attempt to ruin his program, a program which he could not obtain without the support of the conservative Republicans. Bristow did not know that Taft, at times, was having to press the conservatives to support his program. Like many midwesterners Bristow always thought he saw an alliance of the conservatives and the President with monopolies and vested interests. It seemed clear to him that the Republican party must be freed from the domination of the conservative wing. Consequently, for four years the split widened within the party and, where harmony could have prevailed, party discord flourished. Bristow had been slow to adopt the progressive position, but, once converted, he was impatient and critical of any delay. President Taft, who also desired reforms, was perhaps overly cautious and disliked political controversy.

When the Mann-Elkins bill for the control of railroad abuses came before the Senate, Bristow opposed it for two major reasons. He felt that the proposed commerce court would weaken the work of the Interstate Commerce Commission, especially if the commission were denied legal representation before the court; such a denial was actually proposed by the conservatives. He also believed that the new court would be packed with men supported or named by the railway interests. Bristow made a masterly attack on the long- and short-haul abuses in interstate commerce. In two days he presented some fifteen amendments to the commerce bill. Most of these proposals were minor, but they added to the uncertainty of President Taft's program.[32]

Taft was furious at the insurgent position. He wrote to his brother Horace: "Cummins, LaFollette, Dolliver, Clapp and Bristow are five Senators who are determined to be as bitter as they can against the administration and to defeat everything the administration seeks. Their method of defeat is to attempt to load down the legislation with measures so extremely radical that the sensible members of Congress won't vote for them, or that I shall have to veto, if they come to me."[33] Neither Taft nor the insurgents were completely satisfied with the commerce bill, but Bristow gave his support to the measure in its final form.

President Taft and the liberal Republicans desired the establishment of a national postal savings bank. The proposal was important to Taft "because it promotes thrift among the poor, who are not disposed to deposit money in the bank because they distrust the banks, and so they spend money which they would otherwise save."[34] The President worked hard for the measure in the face of strong banker and investment-house opposition to the proposal.[35] Bristow, too, wanted the postal savings bank. He had seen the failure of the states to adopt adequate guarantee-of-deposit laws, and he was ever aware of the hostility of the small depositor to the service charges levied by the banks. He had observed the gravitation of money to the East and the seasonal lack of a supply of money in the West. The insurgents amended the Senate bill to force the postal savings banks to deposit their money in local banks, introducing severe restrictions on the removal of the deposits.[36] Once again it appeared that Taft and Bristow were at opposite poles. Taft felt he would be compelled to veto the bill as it was passed by the Senate because it was ruined by the insurgents' amendments, especially a Cummins amendment that would have prevented the withdrawing of local funds except in case of war. He felt that the insurgents "were utterly oblivious to the importance of maintaining the credit of the government, or of doing anything except filling the coffers of the country banks with these collections."[37] The insurgents' amendments were finally defeated, and on June 11, 1910, Taft wrote, "I am pleased as punch about the postal savings bill."[38] At first only one post office in each state or territory was designated as a federal depository, but by 1916 some 8,421 depositories were established at 7,701 post offices and 720 branch offices. In addition the national supervising board of trustees made many deposits of postal savings funds in the local banks.

Of the early proposals by President Taft, Bristow was most interested in a parcel post system. He had seen the experiments with rural and city mail deliveries while serving in the Post Office Department, and he sensed the need of his rural constituents for protection from high express rates. For years he had urged the adoption of a parcel post system. He had gone so far as to propose that each post office become a zone center for the delivery of parcels to the rural areas. Bristow, Dolliver, and other insurgents had found strong opposition among local merchants to parcel post.[39] It was hard to reconcile local and national interests. Any national system with no regulation of mailing distances would give the catalogue and department stores too great an advantage over the local merchants. Bristow had stood against any system that would enable these business agencies to distribute goods more cheaply than the local merchants.[40] Gradually, however, Bristow joined the forces advocating a national system, helping to work out a zoning arrangement. In doing so he made a major contribution. Equity might not be obtainable for all concerned, but the Bourne-Bristow plan of a zone system with eight zones and graduated postal rates was adopted by Congress in August, 1912.[41] Bristow described this work as the "most trying" of his experiences in the Senate, but he justified his support of parcel post on the grounds that he could not stand in the way of "the currents of modern business life."[42] While working for the parcel post system, Bristow also used his influence to keep low postal rates for second-class mail. He felt that the "interests" wanted to destroy the liberal magazines, which were injurious to their cause.[43]

The various amendments to administration bills and the general tactics of delay widened the breach between the conservatives and the progressives in the Republican party, but the final clash came over the Ballinger-Pinchot controversy. Many liberals had been attracted to the Roosevelt administration by the President's dramatic withdrawal of public lands from private use. Gifford Pinchot, the director of the Bureau of Forestry, became one of the greatest contemporary champions of conservation. Bristow, who had worked with conservation and irrigation in his own state, had become an ardent advocate of Roosevelt's policies, but conservation had made many foes throughout the West, especially among the lumbermen, farmers, miners, and cattlemen who were being denied the riches in the public domain. When President Taft replaced Secretary of Interior Harry Garfield with Richard A. Ballinger, the conservationists, especially Pinchot, were unhappy. Taft and Ballinger startled the conservationists when they made available for private use over one million acres which Roosevelt had withdrawn around water power sites for use as ranger stations. This action made Roosevelt's withdrawal appear illegal. For nearly two years Louis R. Glavis had been conducting an assigned investigation of the Cunningham interests in the use of coal lands in Alaska, trying to find proof that would tie the Cunningham interests to the Morgan-Guggenheim syndicate.[44] When his findings became public, he was removed from his job on the grounds that the investigation had been too slow. Meanwhile, Pinchot was flooding the liberal press and bombarding the progressives with information that made it appear that Taft and Ballinger were against sound conservation practices. Pinchot was determined to force a congressional investigation of the administration's conduct. An indictment by Pinchot was read on the Senate floor by Senator Dolliver as an open letter from the forester. Soon Secretary of Agriculture Wilson asked for Pinchot's resignation, and the battle was on in earnest.

Always loyal to conservation, Bristow had applauded Taft's early stand on irrigation.[45] When the Ballinger-Pinchot controversy arose, Bristow wrote that the denunciation of Ballinger "was a bit severe."[46] But soon the progressives were aware that the issue was not over conservation alone. It had become a clash between progressives and conservatives, conservationists and anti-conservationists, and pro-Roosevelt and anti-Roosevelt men. When Dolliver read Pinchot's letter, Bristow described it as a "masterstroke" of defiance. He could not see how the President and the rest of the conservatives would "get over it."[47] He was certain that the conservatives were out to destroy both Pinchot and Glavis. Actually there was little choice for the progressives but to align themselves on the side of Pinchot. Henry Wallace of Iowa stated their position when he wrote to Senator Dolliver: "As it is now every mother's son of you who have dared to protest against the present rule in the Republican Party will suffer the fate of Pinchot. You must hang together or hang separately." He suggested to Dolliver that the Democrats would stand by Pinchot and that the "Progressive politicians must do so or be crushed out."[48] To Bristow, Ballingerism was only one symptom of a great national disease: the special interests. When the Cunningham coal claims were canceled in Alaska, Bristow called for the reinstatement of Glavis and Pinchot, although he knew the latter would not return to serve under Taft. Bristow declared that the cancellation was an official confirmation of Pinchot's position and an unqualified vindication of Glavis.[49] The Ballinger-Pinchot controversy seemed to be proof to the conservationists and progressives of Taft's great faculty for blundering, and it left political wounds that the administration could never heal. Bristow's stand on the issue no doubt led to his inclusion among the Kansas delegation that was invited to visit Theodore Roosevelt in the summer of 1910.

The Ballinger-Pinchot affair drove many liberals from the support of President Taft, and, in turn, the midwestern Republican liberals found that Taft would not follow their recommendations on the disposal of patronage positions. From the beginning of his term in the Senate, Bristow was locked in a bitter contest with Senator Curtis over filling federal vacancies in Kansas. The conservative Republicans had captured some of the party offices at the Kansas Day celebration in 1910, and Senator Curtis took it upon himself to prove to President Taft that the Bristow forces had no power in state affairs. When the insurgents began a vigorous opposition to the Taft program, Curtis made a bitter attack on "Joe" for not supporting the administration. Governor Stubbs and Bristow backed Robert Stone for a vacancy in the Department of Justice, but when Taft found the Kansas delegation in disagreement, he withdrew the nomination and Kansas lost the position.[50] Bristow opposed the reappointment of Harry T. Bone, a Curtis man and follower of former Senator Long, and recommended for district attorney W. S. Huggins of Emporia instead.[51] After several months Curtis and Bristow visited with Taft; the President promised to divide the positions, but Curtis refused to agree. In December, 1909, Bristow wrote that he was in doubt about whether he would get any positions. The chief vacancies in dispute were a pension agent, a collector of internal revenue, and a United States marshal. Bristow wanted a strong man in the revenue service, but he wrote to Arthur Capper that he would not sacrifice his political program for patronage.[52] The settlement was finally reached in July, 1911, when Bristow's friend John R. Harrison was appointed as U.S. marshal and Curtis secured the appointments of A. W. Smith, a veteran, as pension agent and of Fremont Leidy, a former state senator, as collector of internal revenue. As a rule, President Taft followed the recommendations of members of the House in filling vacancies in the postal service, but Bristow blocked the confirmation of the reappointment of Thomas D. Fitzpatrick as postmaster of Salina and secured the position for his chief local supporter, George M. Hull.[53]

One nonpolitical appointment undoubtedly brought great

satisfaction to Senator Bristow in later years. On August 20, 1910, a young man from Abilene, Kansas, Dwight Eisenhower, applied for an appointment at either Annapolis or West Point.[54] On August 23, George C. Sterl of Abilene strongly recommended Eisenhower for Annapolis.[55] Bristow asked the state superintendent of public schools, E. T. Fairchild, to give the first screening examination to the candidates for Annapolis and West Point. George Pulsifer scored 89½ per cent and Eisenhower scored 87¼ per cent. Eisenhower was strong in mathematics and weak in history. Bristow selected Eisenhower for West Point, notifying him of his appointment on October 24, 1910. Thus Eisenhower, future commander of the armies of many nations, came within a man of being a naval officer. In describing the selection of Eisenhower, Bristow wrote, "I have been very favorably impressed with his character and qualifications."[56]

When President Taft started to work for a reciprocal trade treaty with Canada, he caused considerable consternation among the congressmen from the farm states. On February 14, 1911, Bristow wrote that Taft had "flopped from an ultra-high protectionist to a free trader."[57] A few days earlier he had written to Ida M. Tarbell that he had not made up his mind on the proposal since it had the "same marks of dishonesty that all these measures have."[58] But by April, Bristow had joined with LaFollette and Cummins in sponsoring a series of amendments to the reciprocal trade bill, aimed at lowering the rates on manufactured goods. Bristow again attacked the sugar and lead rates and renewed his drive against the Dutch standard. On July 13 and 14 he spoke in the Senate against the bill, declaring that it took the tariff off articles not controlled by the trusts while retaining high rates on those controlled by the trusts. He also argued that the rates on agricultural products were too low and would place the farmer in a precarious position.[59] He wrote to his friend John Harrison that "no one will deny that the duties on agricultural products are largely *buncombe*," but that some duty ought to be retained on wheat, oats, and barley.[60] He accused the newspapers of supporting Taft in order to obtain free newsprint. The conservative

Republicans joined with the Democrats and defeated all the progressive amendments to the Senate bill. In a sense Taft had gotten even with the western insurgents.[61] Two characteristics of the progressives were shown in this struggle, their assumed loyalty to agrarian interests and their intense nationalism. Bristow expressed great pleasure when the Canadian government rejected the reciprocity proposal.[62]

It is difficult to evaluate Bristow's contribution to the legislative program. He was always alert to the needs of his own area, and he constantly tried to curtail the grip of vested interest groups on national affairs. His progressivism and sense of political timing is shown in his introduction on January 6, 1913, of a bill to create a powerful national industrial commission. His proposed commission was in many ways similar to the Federal Trade Commission that was shortly afterwards established under President Wilson, and it contained some degree of control over investment practices that were not corrected until the 1930's.[63]

Fairly successful as a legislator, he played an even more effective role as a campaigner in the elections of 1910 and 1912. He set the stage for the campaigns in a letter to Arthur S. Hemingway of the Chicago *Tribune* when the latter asked Bristow in 1910 if he was an insurgent. Bristow replied:

> I suppose I am styled as an "insurgent" Republican because I voted against the Payne-Aldrich tariff bill. I voted against that bill because it was framed *more* with a view of benefiting certain manufacturing interests and monopolies than to contribute to the general welfare of the American people. I am opposed to all legislation of that kind, whether it be a railroad bill, a currency measure, or a tariff bill, and in this respect I disagree with the Republican organization of the Senate and therefore vote independently; and I suppose for these reasons I am styled an "insurgent."[64]

Two Campaigns

Theodore Roosevelt may have coined the phrase "the strenuous life," but examination of the busy life led by the progressive Republicans during the campaigns of 1910 and 1912 would convince even the most skeptical that Roosevelt was not the sole practitioner. While on duty in Washington, the insurgents attended strategy conferences, sought out press interviews, wrote articles for reform periodicals, and often spent weekends on speaking tours. As soon as Congress adjourned, the members hurried home, usually taking with them a part of their secretarial staffs to man the headquarters in their home towns. Frequent tours were made throughout the home states with an occasional congressional junket added. One of Senator Bristow's favorite committee excursions was to Panama to inspect the progress on the construction of the Panama Canal. At home there were many letters to be written—arranging for state conventions, drafting state party platforms, and mending political fences. By midsummer of 1910, the insurgent Republicans were well into their stride. Each of them was dedicated to the task of carrying the reform issues to the people, and each was determined to use all his political strength to wrest the control of the Republican party from the conservatives.

Had it not been for the nearly magical power of the Chautauqua circuit, far less would have been accomplished. The insurgent congressmen did not have support from party funds, and their salaries were inadequate to pay for their extensive campaigns. The income from the speeches made on the circuit subsidized the spread of progressive principles. Senator Bristow was often scheduled several months ahead for his Chautauqua appearances, and much of his effective campaigning took place on the Chautauqua and Lyceum platforms. Dolliver, Norris, Beveridge, Cummins, Clapp, and many others reached the people in the same manner. Even the conservative Republicans used the same methods, often timing their schedules to attempt effective rebuttals to the liberal arguments.

Probably no two Republicans came to progressivism by the same route. Men like Cummins, Norris, and Bristow had been drawn into the movement by their support of popular reforms. Others, like Senator Dolliver of Iowa, whom Garret A. Hobart had greeted "as an old spell-binder whose wit and wisdom has always had the power to make votes,"[1] claimed a sudden conversion to progressivism. Actually, Dolliver had been blessed with a fairly liberal past, but his conversion—or better still emancipation—which he openly proclaimed, caught the public fancy in Iowa and neighboring states.[2] Senator Beveridge, during a summer stay in Dublin, New Hampshire, described Dolliver's conversion to Winston Churchill, the author; John Bass, the famous war correspondent; and his brother, Robert Bass, who was an insurgent candidate for the governorship of New Hampshire. Beveridge wrote that Churchill "whooped like a wild Indian" when Beveridge told him that Dolliver had declared that the old Negro slave was not more emancipated forty years before than he (Dolliver) had been during the last year.[3]

Joseph Bristow's term in the Senate was not due to expire until 1915, but he campaigned heroically on behalf of many other Republicans in 1910 and 1912. In January, 1910, he spoke in New York and Massachusetts, and when he returned to Washington, he told the Massachusetts politicos that it would be as easy for the progressive Republicans to defeat Senator Lodge as it had been for him to defeat Senator Long in 1908. The results of the early election in Massachusetts, which favored the liberals, stunned the standpat crowd in Washington.[4] In March the conservatives sent Congressman Duncan E. McKinlay to Kansas to still the voices of progressivism, but Stubbs, White, Murdock, Madison, Allen, and Bristow were the progressive leaders in Kansas, and none was easily silenced. By early June, Bristow was hounding the editors of the area's leading newspapers, the Kansas City *Star,* the Topeka *Capital,* and the Emporia *Gazette,* to begin "a hot campaign along national lines." He urged them to take up and discuss the tariff and railroad bills and progressive policies in general: "anti-Cannonism, anti-Aldrichism, and anti-Reaction." To White he wrote, "Kansas is for progress, not reaction. Kansas is out to lead, and not follow in this great progressive movement."[5] And he admonished the Emporia editor not "to fritter away" the campaign on small issues, such as salaries and duties of guards of the state prisons. Bristow wrote to J. A. Kimball of Salina, a Bristow supporter, "I never have been in favor of the initiative and referendum and have doubted as to recall; but eight years of experience in Oregon has convinced me that it is wise in a state like ours." He added that he believed in government by the people and felt that "you can trust them."[6] Later, in July, he wrote a five-page letter to White urging him to support the Oregon system. He predicted the value of the Oregon system in the state, "Let all the progressives concentrate on that issue and you will skin the reactionaries alive."[7]

The elections of 1910 and 1912 brought Bristow to the zenith of his power and influence. There were requests for him to speak from Maine to California. Wherever critical political contests occurred, he was asked to enter. Frequently a group of the progressives would barnstorm a state for a week or ten days, and as a campaigner Bristow won a leading place among the insurgent Republicans. After Bristow's famous attack on Senator Aldrich in Winfield, Kansas, in early July, Senator Beveridge wrote: "You have strangely captured the imagination and conscience of the people. I know only one man that has captured it more in the last twelve months and that is Dolliver. But of course Dolliver is the Mirabeau of our cause. LaFollette and Cummins have been establishing their hold for years and years, but you have blazed suddenly athwart the public conscience and the public mind."[8] In August, Beveridge wrote: "You are doing very, very wonderful work indeed. Your industry, your intense earnestness, your careful and studious investigations have made you one of the most effective men on the American political platform."[9]

A highlight for Bristow, early in the primary campaign, was a telephone call from Gibson Gardner inviting Bristow to lunch with Colonel Roosevelt at Oyster Bay. The former President had just returned from abroad and was itching to feel out the temper of national politics. On July 2, 1910, Bristow and the two Kansas insurgent congressmen, Murdock and Madison, held a three-hour conference with Roosevelt. Political reporters had many interpretations of the significance of the meeting, which had been headlined in the state press with "Kansas Insurgents Storm Sagamore Hill." Bristow had doubts about the degree of T. R.'s liberalism. On the day before the visit, Bristow had written Senator Bourne that Colonel Roosevelt "will not go as far as you and I on popular government."[10] Hamilton Fish wrote George Norris that, judging from the papers, "the visit of Bristow, Madison and Murdock to Oyster Bay was very successful" and they received a hearty welcome.[11] Bristow found that T. R. was "very encouraging indeed" and that he expressed sympathy for the things for which they were contending. Roosevelt made it clear that he could not criticize President Taft personally, but that he would take a positive stand on progressive ideas in his future speeches.[12]

In describing the visit to Richard L. Jones of Greenwich, Connecticut, Bristow wrote that Roosevelt was not at all satisfied with the Taft administration. The impression made upon Bristow was that the former President was "more advanced and radical in his progressive ideas than he has ever been before."[13] During the visit final plans were made for Roosevelt to deliver a speech at the dedication of the John Brown Memorial Park at Osawatomie,

Kansas, to be held August 30–31; this was to be one of the great conclaves of the insurgents. President Taft's administrative re-action to the Oyster Bay visit was best shown in a letter to all the members of his cabinet asking them not to say anything on the subject so as not to create a situation.[14]

Bristow kept up his correspondence with Roosevelt during the campaign. He argued that many progressives were for the restoration of more competition in business and expressed fears that in the scheme of government regulation of business there was a grave danger that big business might more likely control the government than the government control big business.[15]

After the Oyster Bay visit Bristow started on his state cam-paign tour. On July 9, from the Chautauqua platform at Winfield, he made a bitter attack on Senator Aldrich and his tariff policy. He charged that Aldrich, his son, and several key industrial friends had profited enormously from the rubber schedules in the Payne-Aldrich Tariff Act. Bristow had some facts about a new cartel, the Intercontinental Rubber Company. The new company, dealing in crude rubber, had paid in the first 314 days of its exist-ence dividends reaching 18.2 per cent. Such names as Baruch, Guggenheim, Martin, Ryan, and Sproule were included by Bris-tow, who declared that Aldrich was the central interest behind the syndicate.[16] Bristow had spoken from rough notes, but afterwards it was necessary to do more research and put the speech in manu-script form.[17] Ida Tarbell assisted Bristow in proving his accusa-tions and from Poor's *Annual of Industrials,* the *Wall Street Journal,* and *Moody's Manual* helped to confirm the facts.[18] Bristow's speech with the additions was widely circulated in mid-western newspapers. Aldrich at first declared that the accusations were a pack of lies, and he later denied that he held such invest-ments.[19] The controversy raged until late August. On August 18, 1910, Bristow wrote Beveridge, "I have got the goods on Aldrich. . . . He doesn't deny a single fact that I declare."[20] Eventually, Aldrich admitted he owned rubber shares outside the United States but insisted that his ownership did not control the manu-factured price of rubber. Bristow believed that this attack on a vested interest had a strong impact on the outcome of the primary election in 1910, and it took away much of Aldrich's effectiveness in the Senate.[21]

The conservative Republicans hurried speakers to Kansas to defend Aldrich, with "Uncle Joe" Cannon leading the pack. Bristow wrote Senator Dolliver that "we are having a hot contest in Kansas. Old Cannon has been here storming like a mad bull; denouncing me as a liar, a Democrat, a demagogue, and everything else." Cannon was scheduled to speak for ten days, but the hot weather "tuckered him out" and he left early for Lake Mackinac to recuperate. Ironically, and to Bristow's delight, the Chautauqua committee engaged "Vic" Murdock to substitute for Cannon.[22]

The campaign was indeed strenuous in Kansas. "I never had such meetings in my life as I am having in Kansas," Bristow wrote Dolliver, and he invited the Iowa senator to come down and get a little Kansas "insurgent enthusiasm."[23] Charles Towne, a lawyer from New York, wrote Dolliver that "Bristow has been handing Uncle Joe some hot ones lately. I am enjoying the spectacle."[24] On August 2, Bristow wrote Senator Thomas P. Gore that the campaign had been almost beyond endurance on account of the terrible heat. Bristow said he would like to have a rest, but he had promised to go to Wisconsin to help "Bob" LaFollette.[25] On the same day he wrote to John Hannan, who was making the Wisconsin arrangements, not to bill him for two speeches in one day. "I am just about played out, my throat is in bad shape," he wrote. He had been speaking often twice a day with the mercury ranging from 105 to 110 degrees.[26]

The results of the second primary election in Kansas were indeed gratifying to the liberal forces in the Republican party. In brief notes to Cummins, Beveridge, LaFollette, and Clapp, Bristow reported on August 3 that the liberals had carried the state for Governor Stubbs by an approximately thirty thousand majority and that they had defeated four of the six "reactionary" congressmen. Stubbs had carried all but five counties, and many liberals had been nominated for minor offices in the state. Bristow felt that the leading issue had been the tariff, with railroads next.[27]

William Allen White saw a lighter side to the victory. Senator Dolliver had not been able to come to Kansas to help in the primary campaign. On August 9, White wrote to Dolliver, "You were dead right. We didn't need you. Cannon did the business."[28]

On August 5, Bristow wrote to Colonel Nelson, editor of the Kansas City *Star,* that the *Star* had contributed more to the victory "than all the rest of us combined." He stressed the national impact of the Kansas election: "The result of this election ought to convince Colonel Roosevelt that he can't straddle the tariff question. He has to face the proposition square-toed, and not permit Lodge and Root to blind him, or he will go down; because this movement is bigger than any man."[29]

At the close of the Kansas campaign, Bristow wrote in several letters to his associates of his plans to help LaFollette. From all indications LaFollette was in trouble and needed assistance. The banking interests were organizing against him, but more serious was the fact that LaFollette was ill and was facing major surgery. Early in August the leaders of progressivism, Dolliver, Cummins, Clapp, Bristow, Borah, Pinchot, Garfield, Lindsey, Heney, Norris, and others descended on the state of Wisconsin and made 180 speeches in seven days for LaFollette and the liberal congressional candidates. Bristow continued his attack on Aldrich, accusing the conservative senator of violating political decency and honesty and of using his office for personal gain.[30]

LaFollette carried the state by 102,000 votes, and 80 out of 118 members of the legislature were pledged to his support. Bristow was deeply impressed by the Wisconsin venture. "It is a real inspiration to a man in public life to go up into Wisconsin and come in contact with LaFollette's friends," he wrote to Beveridge. "They call him 'our Bob'—sometimes 'our little Bob'—with an affectionate regard that is rare in human experience."[31] John Hannan wrote Dolliver in August that Senator Bristow had done a fine job in behalf of LaFollette.[32] LaFollette described the victory to Beveridge in September: "It was a hard fight in Wisconsin. The figures showing the popular vote tell the story. Had it not been for the good work of our friends, Senators Cummins, Dolliver, Bristow, Clapp, and Borah, and George L. Record and others it would have been impossible to roll up the great popular majority of 102,000."[33]

Iowa progressives were equally pleased with the outcome of the Republican convention in their state, where the Dolliver and Cummins forces were swept into the control of the party, and a liberal platform was adopted. Beveridge wrote to Cummins that the action of the Iowa convention, coming immediately after Bristow's triumph in the Kansas primaries, would have a "far reaching effect." He declared that the reactionary leaders "cannot fail to understand the power as well as the significance of this great movement for common sense and common honesty."[34]

Meanwhile, the Midwest progressives made plans to meet at Osawatomie for the dedication of the John Brown Memorial Park on August 30 and 31, knowing that Theodore Roosevelt would be one of the principal speakers. The dedication ceremonies drew men and women from all walks of life. Veterans of the Civil War from Kansas and the neighboring states were given a prominent place. Here the conservative Charles Curtis sat on the same platform with the liberal Bristow, and later the two attended the banquet. One could read many things into the dedication. Certainly it was a great tribute to the part played by Kansans in the Civil War. Moreover, the attendance of the progressive Republicans pointed to the fact that the Midwest was to become a champion of new political issues. And before the ceremonies ended, Theodore Roosevelt had presented a new platform for the Republican party. A careful study of the ideas presented by Roosevelt in his New Nationalism will show that the former President borrowed heavily from the Iowa and Kansas platforms; the latter had been drafted by William Allen White and was regarded as sound progressivism decades later in the days of the New Deal.

The progressive spirit was indeed high in Kansas following

Roosevelt's address. When Congressman Ed Madison spoke at the University of Kansas, the students greeted him with a "new yell":

> *Stubbs, Madison*
> *Murdock, Bristow*
> *We'll sweep the land*
> *From Maine to Frisco.*[35]

Bristow continued his crowded campaign schedule until the fall election. At the suggestion of White, he spent about ten days in Colorado supporting "young Vincent," George S. Vincent, who had dared to stand up against Senator Simon Guggenheim. He observed that Colorado politically was "the rottenest place I have yet found."[36] After a short trip to Illinois, Bristow was convinced that the Republicans were afraid of new ideas. When he joined other progressives to assist Beveridge in Indiana, he was not satisfied with the Indiana meetings and predicted privately that Beveridge would be defeated.[37] Beveridge was in fact narrowly defeated in November; he estimated that a change of only six to eight hundred votes could have given him a majority in the state legislature.[38] When William Jennings Bryan came to Kansas to campaign against the progressive nominees, Bristow sensed the irony of it and wrote Beveridge, "Isn't it a strange thing that Bryan should come to Kansas and speak against the progressive nominees instead of the stand patters."[39] In October he wrote to Ray Stannard Baker, the journalist, pointing out that it was inconsistent for Theodore Roosevelt to throw his weight to Lodge and to "speak in highest praise of Beveridge and myself."[40] Throughout the campaign Bristow spoke some two hundred times and never missed a date. There is no doubt that he was a major force in the liberal victories in the 1910 elections.

The liberal forces were dealt a serious blow by the death of Senator Dolliver on October 15, 1910. In a letter to Albert Shaw, the editor of the *Review of Reviews,* Bristow wrote that he considered Dolliver the "greatest debater in the American Congress." He described Dolliver's attractive personality and said that the

Iowa senator was loved by everybody in the Senate, unless it was
Senator Aldrich, who seemed to dislike him. Bristow assessed
Dolliver's death as "an irreparable loss to the great progressive
movement."[41]

The strenuous campaigning during 1910 had heavily taxed
Bristow's health. He was never a strong man physically, and he
often pushed himself too hard. For years poor eyesight limited
his reading, and he was frequently bothered by a weak stomach.
Fortunately, he found relief for his stomach by eating the new
foods prepared at Battle Creek, Michigan. He ordered large
quantities of these prepared cereals, which he referred to as his
"Battle Creek diet." He frequently worried over the debts on his
Salina projects, and in 1911 he transferred his speaking arrangements to the Redpath Chautauqua Company, because this company paid him more than he had been receiving. In 1911 he owed
$2,500 on his house, $4,000 on his farm, and $2,400 on the *Journal*
building. He had high standards for his paper and poured back
all the profits from the *Journal* for modern equipment.[42] He was
deeply disturbed in February, 1911, when an attempt was made to
unionize the *Journal* staff. He urged his manager to hold the line
and not increase wages. After a two months' struggle, in which
some of the employees went on strike, the manager defeated
unionization and reduced the monthly payroll by some $325.[43]
Bristow's position on the unionization of his own business gave
his critics an open opportunity to call him an anti-labor senator.

Under heavy pressure from his congressional friends, he took
up golf for relaxation, joining the Columbia Country Club in
Chevy Chase, Maryland. He enjoyed the game, and when he
went to Salina during the summer he joined the local club. On
one occasion he invited Norris Brown of Nebraska to join him in
a game at Salina. He furnished Brown a copy of a score of ninety-
four on eighteen holes, certified by the Honorable Jonathan
Bourne and the Honorable Joseph M. Nixon.[44] In a letter to
Brown's daughter Lucile, he boasted that her father could only
beat him on his "bad days," and he jokingly accused Brown of

complimenting the good players so that he felt much better when he defeated them.[45]

During the summer of 1911, Bristow purchased a home in Washington, near the Connecticut Avenue bridge. In a letter to his son Frank, he called it a "neat little house of nine rooms—near enough to the zoo to hear the lions grunt and the coyotes bark." In a five-minute walk he could get out into the forest, but he was still only "30 min. from his office." The Connecticut Avenue streetcar line was 150 feet from his door, and he could reach the country club in eighteen minutes.[46]

In October, 1911, Bristow joined Senator Cummins on a trip to the Panama Canal Zone. Mrs. Bristow and Bristow's secretary, C. C. Hardy, accompanied the senators. Hardy had been married just before the tour, so his bride was included on what the Hardys called their honeymoon cruise.[47] During the trip Bristow and Cummins drafted a bill for the government of the Canal Zone.

Private activities by no means diverted Bristow's attention from politics, and he was deeply involved in the great progressive movement that surged ahead prior to the election of 1912. In January, 1911, he took an active part in the formation of the National Progressive Republican League, and he served as a member of the league's executive committee.[48] By May 1 he was convinced that the renomination of President Taft would mean the election of a Democrat for President.[49] On May 2 he sent Theodore Roosevelt a copy of a poll that had been conducted by the *Missouri Valley Farmer,* a Capper publication, which showed Taft only three hundred votes ahead of Eugene Debs and indicated that the President stood in fourth place among the first choices.[50] In June, Bristow privately endorsed Arthur Capper as the Republican candidate for the Kansas governorship, saying, "Capper is as strong a man as we could run."[51] He wrote Henry Allen that he had tried to impress Capper that the only way to be elected governor was to get the people to think that as a candidate he was much more progressive than Taft.[52] Bristow wanted a progressive Republican party in Kansas, but he knew there were many conservatives who would not step aside. He sensed the same danger for liberal Democrats in Kansas.[53] During the month of May, Bristow sent out over two hundred letters trying to build a solid bloc of liberal Republicans for committeemen in the state.

Bristow constantly fretted over the fact that Kansas progressives were not in the open fighting for progressive principles such as the presidential primary and the Oregon system. He urged White and others to take a more progressive stand, and he criticized Governor Stubbs because he had not been able to build a more effective organization.[54] But in outward appearances Bristow did not reveal the disharmony in his party. He invited President Taft to be the speaker at the installation of Wilbur N. Mason as president of Baker University.[55] When Taft toured the state for four days in September, 1911, Bristow traveled three days with the presidential party. But Kansas sentiment had moved well away from Taft by this time. As Bristow described the Taft visit to Henry Allen, "Nobody went crazy or got drunk over Taft's visit to Kansas."[56]

For the national Republican leadership Bristow at first supported Robert M. LaFollette. He was of course deeply indebted to LaFollette for his own political advancement, and he regarded LaFollette as the "greatest constructive statesman in America today."[57] But in August he wrote Harold Chase that he did not think that LaFollette could be nominated, although he had a good following in Kansas. "I would rather fight for LaFollette and lose, than join Taft and win," he declared to Chase.[58] By December, Bristow was expressing his fears that Theodore Roosevelt, who had strong support in the East, would also be able to block LaFollette in the West. Capper felt that Roosevelt would make a better showing in Kansas than LaFollette,[59] and Bristow knew that there were individuals closely associated with LaFollette who were willing to see his organization turned over to Roosevelt, provided that they could control the organization.[60] He complained to Jack Harrison that "Will" White and his literary friends were for Roosevelt because "he runs the government" through them, giving them "fine offices" and conferring with them more than he does with anybody else.[61] On January 31, 1912, he wrote his son, "It looks very much as though Roosevelt will be the nominee. Kansas is overwhelmingly for him."[62] It was hard for the Kansas senator to leave the LaFollette camp, but the tide in his state was against the Wisconsin leader. Bristow was present at the Philadelphia Periodical Publishers' dinner on February 12. He felt that the occasion offered a remarkable opportunity to win an influential audience, but LaFollette failed to grasp it. Bristow realized that LaFollette had not developed the political strength needed, and he decided that he must "forego a personal choice for the good of a great movement."[63]

When the Republican state convention met in May, 1912, Roosevelt was leading Taft seven to one. Eighteen Kansas delegates to the Republican National Convention were pledged to Roosevelt and two to President Taft. Bristow wrote to Fred H. Quincy on May 24: "Taft told a United States Senator this morning before he left for New Jersey that he intended to have the nomination at Chicago; that he was going to take it; that he didn't care a d——m what happened after the convention, he intended to have the nomination."[64]

Taft won his nomination at Chicago in a convention that Bristow described as "chaotic," and the standpatters, according to Bristow, were now "scared to death" because Roosevelt was going to run as an independent.[65] Most of the progressives in Kansas immediately swung to Roosevelt. William Allen White resigned his position on the Republican National Committee and took up the leadership of the third-party forces. And Henry Allen, who had gone to the regular Republican convention with a well-prepared seconding speech for Roosevelt, had to return later to the Bull Moose convention to practice his oratory.

Bristow was assured at the Chicago convention that a third party would not interfere with political conditions in Kansas, that third parties would be placed on a separate ballot only in the conservative states.[66] Such was not the case, and in the November election Kansas had three sets of presidential electors.

Bristow toured Europe in July and August, and when he returned from Europe, he campaigned as actively as he had in

1910. Having officially endorsed Arthur Capper and the Progressive party candidates on August 1, 1912,[67] Bristow delivered most of his speeches in Kansas, where the three most popular speakers were Stubbs, Bristow, and Allen. Bristow had written to T. R. in May, outlining his position on progressive issues. In his letter he emphasized the need for a parcel post based on a zoning system. Although the income tax was more popular than the inheritance tax, he endorsed both, but gave his opinion that the latter was easier to collect. He supported Senator Newland's proposed program for the federal construction of several dams in the present Tennessee Valley area and urged federal aid to both water and rail transportation to tap the inexhaustible resources of Alaska.[68] Bristow interpreted the nomination of Wilson by the Democrats as a serious blow to the progressive Republicans. He felt that many Democratic liberals who might have voted for Roosevelt would now remain in the party and support Wilson, for Wilson represented "all that the progressive Republicans stood for."[69] In October he predicted that the Republican split would enable Wilson to carry Kansas and give the state a winning Democratic ticket.[70] Roosevelt made two visits to Kansas during the campaign, but the Bull Moosers failed to win the state.

Woodrow Wilson won the electoral vote in Kansas, and the Republican split brought the Democrats into power. William H. Thompson, a Democrat, became a United States senator. George H. Hodges won the governorship over Arthur Capper by twenty-nine votes.[71] As for the House of Representatives, White wrote to Roosevelt that the progressives had lost "everything" but Murdock.[72] For the first time in the history of the state, the Democrats won a majority in both houses of the state legislature. The Kansas progressives had spent $11,000 on the campaign and had $800 left with which, according to White, they could start a new organization.[73]

In the hour of defeat post-mortems are not always accurate, but emotions are strong. When F. M. Lockard wrote to Bristow that Roosevelt had destroyed the Republican party, Bristow replied: "You are entirely mistaken . . . . Taft and his gang of reactionary politicians are the ones who have destroyed it."[74] Bristow insisted that if Taft had supported the progressive issues in Congress he would have been "triumphantly re-elected." William Allen White, whose enthusiasm often clouded his judgment, moved quickly to form a Progressive party in the state, and he pressed "Joe" to lead the movement. Beveridge joined White and urged him to encourage Bristow and Stubbs to come out squarely for a Progressive party.[75] Roosevelt was equally anxious, and on November 15 he wrote to Bristow: "It may well be that you have the most responsible task that falls to any man in the Progressive Party during the next four years, for it seems to me we must look to you to lead the Progressives in the Senate in the effort to get embodied into law all the measures promised in our national platform. I very earnestly hope that you will be able to put the Progressive organization on a permanent basis."[76] Roosevelt urged Bristow to bring Murdock, Norris, and one or two other progressive Republicans to see him in New York when Bristow came east in December.

Bristow refused to take the lead in the formation of a new party. It looked to him as if the Kansas Republicans were moving farther apart instead of closer. He urged White to work through progressive clubs rather than through a third party, as there were thousands of progressives in Kansas who were unwilling to say they were no longer Republicans.[77] Bristow held to this position, and White went his own way, a way which defeated Joe Bristow in the election of 1914.

The Wilson Years

Senator Joseph Bristow observed closely the political transition from President Taft's administration to Woodrow Wilson's. With many other Republicans he had gone to the Democratic National Convention in Baltimore in June, 1912. From Baltimore he reported to the Kansas press on the strength and the new leadership of the opposition party. With the nomination of Wilson, Bristow and other observers knew that the champion of the New Freedom would attract many liberal votes, some no doubt from the ranks of the Republican party. Wilson's spectacular and rapid rise had electrified the nation.

The election in November of 1912 greatly altered the congressional profile. The progressive Republicans had lost Senators Bourne and Dixon, but they had gained Senators Thomas Sterling of South Dakota and George Norris of Nebraska. They hoped that Senator Borah and his colleague, J. H. Brady, would be progressive;[1] and, as always, there was the chance of attracting some of the liberal Democrats in Congress to their cause. Their most important concern was Wilson's position on leading political issues: Was he a conservative or was he a liberal? For over a year and a half Wilson had been campaigning in generalities. Did he have deep and abiding convictions on the issues he had discussed? Clearly the campaign between Roosevelt and Wilson had brought out sharp differences in the means that the two men would advocate for obtaining and enforcing reforms. Roosevelt had demanded strong powers for the national government, while Wilson spoke of states' rights and a return to vague *laissez faire*.[2] The liberal Republicans were unsure of Wilson.

After the election Taft made an onslaught on progressive Republican officeholders, sending many new nominations to the Senate. By the end of January, 1913, a backlog of nearly two-thousand names lay before the Senate for confirmation. The Democrats pretended offense, especially over Taft's changes in the South, and delayed action on the confirmation of positions which they felt rightfully belonged to them.[3] Kansas Republicans seemed to forget that a Democratic senator would handle the federal patronage after March 4, 1913, and they pressed Bristow to support the nomination of several old-guard Republicans as postmasters. Bristow made it clear that he did not intend to infringe upon Senator Thompson's patronage privileges. "I am not a Democrat," he wrote, "and have no right to exert a voice in the selecting of federal officeholders." He declared that he was going "to stand for every good matter in legislation" that Wilson stood for and "oppose every bad thing" he and the Democrats might advocate.[4] He wrote to J. N. Dolley that his attitude on patronage was not one of retaliation towards the old guard in Kansas, but he did not feel called upon to make "any heroic effort" to save these fellows "from the effect of their own work."[5] Later he declared that in patronage matters a Kansas senator undertaking to control a Washington post office appointment was about as helpless as a Chinaman undertaking to become mayor of San Francisco.[6] Bristow felt that Wilson had been more partisan in his appointments than Roosevelt or Taft, and that Secretary of State Bryan was the worst offender in the cabinet, narrow and prejudiced against Republicans and Progressives.[7]

Bristow found it hard to evaluate President Wilson. In the

first two months of his administration, the President had made a very favorable impression upon the country. But Bristow questioned whether Wilson could carry through tariff and currency reform without disrupting the turbulent democracy. On June 12, 1913, Bristow wrote to White that he was still waiting to come to a conclusion about Wilson. According to Bristow, Wilson talked very well—so did Taft. Wilson had a brilliant mind—Taft did not. Wilson impressed Bristow as a man who lacked depth and the determination to work out any great political reforms.[8] The Kansas senator also felt that Bryan was regarded as a potent influence, but that he would become a great disappointment to his friends and the country.[9]

Bristow soon found, during the special session of Congress in 1913, that Wilson did have a grip on his party's members, frequently putting them through their paces like "seals in the vaudeville," and like seals they demanded a reward of fish for their actions.[10] Often the Kansas senator felt the sting of defeat. But Bristow, like modern historians, never found Woodrow Wilson to be a man of deep convictions. In Bristow's letters the new President was described as brilliant, opinionated and egotistical, and unwilling to learn. By 1915 he was writing to Capper that he regarded Wilson as "the most dangerously reactionary of any man who has been in the White House for half a century."[11]

From the beginning of the administration, Bristow was overly critical of President Wilson's policies. As a Republican, he carried the torch of opposition, making certain that the new administration did not appear too liberal: Modern liberalism was supposedly Republican born. Furthermore, Wilson favored a mild internationalism in his handling of foreign affairs, and Bristow, like most progressive Republicans, was a strong nationalist. The early foreign policy of Bryan and Wilson opened a broad area for Bristow's opposition.

Early in the administration Bristow attacked Bryan's absenteeism from the State Department at a time when the United States had pressing problems with Britain, Mexico, and Japan. At Hendersonville, North Carolina, Bryan had announced that as a cabinet member he had to lecture on the Chautauqua platform to maintain his financial position. The statement grew into a serious national incident. Bryan was sharply criticized throughout the country. Bristow joined the critics and took a stand on the Senate floor against the man who sat at the right hand of the President and could not live on a salary of $12,000 a year; this was the man who for many years had been an advocate of Jeffersonian simplicity. Bristow sparked the attack with a Senate resolution calling upon President Wilson to inform the Senate what would be a proper salary to enable the Secretary to live in comfort so that Congress might take immediate steps to relieve the country from the great loss it suffered by being deprived of the services of the present Secretary of State.[12] Democratic senators rallied to Bryan's defense, although the Secretary's claim of personal financial loss had a hollow ring. The debate started with considerable humor, but soon both sides were hitting below the belt. Bristow lightly suggested that Bryan might live within his income if he followed the Kansas doctrine of serving pure spring water rather than nauseating grape juice at mealtimes. When Senator William J. Stone asked Bristow, who had risen in the public eye by way of the Chautaqua platform, if he ever lectured for pay, Bristow replied angrily, "Not while the Senate was in session or public duty required my presence in Washington." Stone rapped Bristow for his absence during the Democratic National Convention in 1912. Bristow replied that the Senate had promised that no important work would be done at the time, but Stone insisted that the Senate passed a $10,000,000 Indian appropriation bill during Bristow's absence. Senator Henry F. Ashurst dug up the old letter that Senator Long had used to prove that Bristow was looking for a soft job when he left the postal service in 1905.[13] The New York *Times* reported that Bryan had been absent one-fourth of his first 134 days in office and that if he continued his lecture schedule, he would have been absent eleven out of twenty-five weeks in office.[14] The Bristow resolution failed by a decidedly partisan vote of forty-one to twenty-nine. Republican Senators Borah and Poindexter voted with the Democrats. Some of Bristow's friends felt he had erred in attacking Bryan,[15] but Bryan did cancel some of his speeches and delivered others without pay. The Bristow-Bryan encounter pushed President Wilson to a sharper defense of his Mexican policy, on which midwestern progressives had already trained their guns.

The Mexican revolution erupted during President Taft's administration, and Senator Bristow had watched the Mexican leaders divide up into opposing groups. He asked how much force it would require to police the country and if it would be possible to organize a stable system of government. He was of the opinion that the United States would eventually be compelled to intervene to preserve order, and he made it clear that our country could not, under any circumstances, permit foreign powers from outside the hemisphere to interfere: The United States must uphold the Monroe Doctrine.[16] Bristow distrusted President Victoriano Huerta. Three days after President Wilson's inauguration Bristow wrote that from what he could learn "this man Huerta is not capable of administering a great country like Mexico." He found Huerta to be a man of "very ordinary ability, pushed by a cruel determination."[17] Bristow supported Wilson's non-recognition policy toward Huerta, but he consistently argued that Venustiano Carranza should be given access to arms. He opposed Wilson's warning to Americans to leave Mexico and urged the administration to hold Mexico accountable for the protection of Americans lives and property under treaty and law.[18] In the Senate, on November 3, 1913, Bristow read a letter from an old friend residing in Mexico, who denounced the current policy of the State Department as being neither peace nor war. At this time Bristow asked that the Mexican factions be allowed "to fight it out" and that some form of American neutrality be decreed that would keep thousands of soldiers on the Texas frontier as a constant irritant to the Mexicans.[19] In a letter to D. A. Valentine on December 13, 1913, he restated his position to the effect that the United States should say to Huerta and Carranza and all the rest, "You fellows fight it out; work out your own salvation." "And I would say to Europe," he wrote, "keep out and let these people alone." Bristow clearly did not want military intervention of any kind in Mexico.[20]

By April of 1914, Bristow felt that the Wilson administration had moved with little success. To Bristow the Tampico affair was ridiculous. President Wilson had become a "two-faced, bungling demagogue" and was using the demand for an apology with a twenty-one gun salute as an effort to do "something spectacular" to recover public opinion because of his "bungling foreign policy."[21] Bristow took Wilson to task for not protesting when hundreds of Americans had been killed and horrible cruelties inflicted upon men, women, and children. Now, when a "few vagrant sailors get into trouble," the President demanded release and apology, sending ten thousand men and nine or ten battleships to compel the Mexican officer to "salute the admiral."[22]

The Tampico incident was followed by the shelling of Veracruz, an event which Bristow declared to be a hostile act against a friendly country.[23] On April 22, Bristow was one of thirteen Republican senators who voted against a resolution justifying the President's use of force in Mexico.[24] He wrote to F. C. Pomeroy on April 23, 1914, "I am afraid that our President has forced us into a war which will not be received with enthusiasm by our people." In Bristow's own words, the attack on "poor old decrepit, strife ridden Mexico," did not fill him with any degree of pride.[25] He was equally hostile to the proposed mediation by the A B C powers. He asked publicly how the United States could arbitrate with "a bandit whom we did not recognize to be anything but a murderer," and he questioned how the A B C nations could use their influence to mediate between the United States and someone whom it recognized only as an individual.[26]

Fortunately for the United States and Mexico, the A B C mediation held the hope of success, but Bristow was unwilling to recognize the fact. Senator Cummins of Iowa, with Borah and Bristow, had bitterly protested Wilson's control over the Senate and had declared that the Mexican policy had made the United States "a laughing stock."[27] Bristow was in hearty agreement with his fellow progressives and described Wilson's Mexican policy as a most infamous chapter in American history. In Bristow's opinion President Wilson had become the "most designing hypocrite, the most conscienceless betrayer of public interest," who had occupied the President's chair since Van Buren.[28]

Bristow's attack on President Wilson's foreign policy reached its height in his opposition to the repeal of the Panama Tolls Act. The Tolls Act, passed during President Taft's administration, had a double purpose. It was a concealed subsidy to coastwise shippers of the United States who planned to use the canal, and it created a competitive situation which might lower the level of the transcontinental railroad rates. When Great Britain protested our narrow interpretation of the Hay-Pauncefote Treaty, President Wilson, seeking an end to hostile foreign criticism and hoping to save our national honor, recommended that Congress repeal the Tolls Act. Wilson's proposal sparked the battle between the nationalists and the internationalists throughout the land.

Once the debate began in Congress, both major parties split. The chauvinistic Beveridge described the political situation in a letter to W. C. Bobbs of the Bobbs-Merrill Publishing Company. According to Beveridge, Wilson had committed a fatal blunder and both Secretary of State Bryan and the President were brazenly breaking platform pledges. He insisted that, while the Republican and Democratic parties were splitting, the Progressive party would be solidly against repeal. Beveridge accused Wilson of scandalously sacrificing the rights of the United States and of favoring the transcontinental railroad interests, which sought to avoid water competition.[29] Bristow's position was similar to Beveridge's. He had been close to the construction of the canal, and he believed its completion would have a decided influence on railroad rates. Early in the debate he produced a campaign speech that Wilson had made to twenty-five hundred farmers in Washington Park, New Jersey, in which the presidential candidate had explained the great advantages of the canal and had endorsed, unequivocally, free tolls for American coastwise shippers.[30] Bristow argued that a precedent had been established in the free use of the Sault Ste Marie Canal and that the construction of the

Panama Canal should not be paid from tolls any more than other costs for defense and commerce. He not only accused Wilson of giving in to American railroad pressure, but he also attacked the British owners of the railroad across the Isthmus of Tehuantepec.[31] He bitterly denounced the Democratic senators who blindly followed Wilson for fear that they would be "turned out into the wilderness for another forty years." Early in the debate he gave his support to the Cummins amendment, which would have set a ceiling on tolls paid by United States' coastwise shippers at one-half the regular tolls.[32]

Senators Lodge and Stone were bitter in their denunciation of Bristow. Lodge held that the United States was obligated to carry out the President's request or face hostility of other nations that might lead to war. Stone hit hard at Bristow's attack on Wilson's integrity, and on one occasion when Bristow moved for adjournment, Stone hissed "filibuster, filibuster."[33]

The editor of the New York *Times* attacked Bristow and Senator James A. O'Gorman for their opposition to repeal. The editor condemned the spirit which existed in Congress, "the pest of politics," and accused Bristow of trying to please the anti-corporation forces in his state in order to win in the coming primary election.[34] Both the Kansas City *Star* and the Topeka *Capital* were supporting the President's stand. No other contest over peacetime foreign policy had been so strained, and in the final Senate vote twenty-four Republicans voted against repeal; Borah, Bristow, Clapp, Cummins, LaFollette, Perkins, Poindexter, and Smoot were among these. In the House of Representatives eleven Progressives, including Victor Murdock from Kansas, voted against the Wilson proposal. The Progressive party split its vote in both houses. The Wilson forces won,[35] and in his opposition to Wilson's proposal, Bristow had created a situation in which few Democrats could rally to his support in the 1914 election.

Bristow's final blast at President Wilson's foreign policy came over the Colombia apology issue. The proposal to pay Colombia $25,000,000 for the loss of Panama was opposed by both Democrats and Republicans. When Theodore Roosevelt's action in the Panamanian revolution was likened to the German attack on Belgium, Bristow sprang to the defense of Roosevelt, declaring that such a comparison was slander bordering on treason. He believed that if the money were ultimately paid, it would be paid to "a lot of bandits who were blackmailing the American people." Bristow praised the Republican filibuster that kept the proposal locked in the Senate Foreign Relations Committee and branded the basic idea a disgrace to the country.[36]

If Senator Bristow had been overly critical of President Wilson's foreign policy, he was in no mood to relax his criticisms on domestic policy. On the tariff issue Bristow was consistent with the position he had held during the Taft administration. He argued that the progressives had stood for the only sensible position in Congress, one in which excessive rates could be destroyed and the protective principle preserved.[37] Early in the new administration Bristow wrote that Wilson was developing the symptoms of a free trader, to the surprise of a number of the insurgents.[38] The new administration was determined to make a public record through tariff reduction, and it had little difficulty in securing the passage of the Underwood-Simmons bill in the House of Representatives. But the delicate Democratic majority in the Senate tempted the Republicans to delay the measure by long debate in hopes that a few Democrats might join them to defeat unsatisfactory schedules, especially free wool and sugar.

Bristow's contributions during the debate were threefold. He was able to put an end to the use of the outdated Dutch standard for sugar tariffs. He joined with LaFollette in a move to require senators to list their business holdings that might be affected by the new tariff proposal; this move resulted in the public exposure of aggressive lobbies working for higher schedules. Finally, he supported the demand for a higher income tax rate.[39] He was defeated in his attempts to secure a gradual reduction of all rates under the careful supervision of a tariff commission and to abolish the corporation tax.[40]

In his opposition to the Underwood-Simmons bill, the Kansas senator knew that he was in disagreement with the editors of the

Kansas City *Star* and the Topeka *Capital,* along with other citizens of the state, but his private mail ran twenty-five to one against the bill.[41] Drought conditions in the state added to Bristow's fear that the bill was too disadvantageous to the farmers. He found 70 per cent of the agricultural and manufactured products in Kansas on the free list, as compared with the national average of 46 per cent, and he predicted the loss to the state of the beet-sugar industry and other small businesses. He was willing to concede that some of the schedules were better than ever before,[42] but he argued against the claim that lower living costs would result from the bill, since most lowered living costs came through business efficiency. All of his arguments were ignored, and Senate insurgency crumbled before the force of Democratic party unity. The Wilson administration not only secured a low tariff, but also freed the Democratic party from the imagined alliance with the commercial trusts and vested interests.

Bristow had worked hard on the tariff, but he found the physical demands made upon him during the preparation of the Glass-Owen banking bill almost unbearable. He was a minority member of the Banking and Currency Committee, which worked for three months on the proposal. Attending both the regular meetings of the Senate and the committee meetings, Bristow often worked from 10:00 A.M. until 11:00 P.M. The currency bill was uppermost in his mind and he described it as a nightmare about which he was thinking and dreaming.[43] Early in the special session of Congress, Wilson had called the committee for a three-hour session and introduced the new proposal. Bristow's reaction was that Wilson knew little about the question, but he had a "fine facility of expression" and could "generalize beautifully." Of the ten members presents, Bristow wrote that only one, Senator Robert L. Owen, agreed with Wilson.[44] He enjoyed the fact that two Democratic senators, James A. Reed and Gilbert M. Hitchcock, had asked many embarrassing questions.

The daily sessions of the committee were filled with controversy. The midwestern Democrats were often in agreement with the midwestern progressives; the proposed Federal Reserve bank system contained many features that Democratic and Republican progressives had advocated for several years, and they tried hard to make it an effective measure. But Wilson would not keep his hands off the committee, and soon another administration measure was moving through the Senate.

Bristow was in the heart of the battle, both in the committee hearings and on the Senate floor. Once again, he stood for the agricultural interests, and he amended the bill to provide for farm mortgages as one basis for Federal Reserve note circulation. He also tried to include measures to secure long-term farm loans from national banks. He stood firm with other midwesterners for political control of the Federal Reserve Board, and he proposed a system of open market operations and a plan similar to the later RFC in which federal loans could be made to an individual borrower. He also favored the idea of credit extension in times of depression but saw dangers in the overuse of such credit.[45] Like other progressives he was afraid that there would be a drain of reserve money from the local to the regional reserve banks, and he worked against any proposal that would strengthen eastern monopoly control of the nation's financial resources. On one occasion he pointed out the need for a federal guarantee deposit law.[46] In a letter to former Senator Joseph Dixon, Bristow wrote that after ten weeks of persistent fighting, the progressives had forced a number of important changes in the bill and would have forced others if the Democrats had not resorted to caucus methods. It was an administration measure, and "any one who votes as a Democrat [against it] will be branded as a traitor."[47]

Bristow's opposition to such administration pressure led to an unwarranted attack on Senator Owen in which Bristow accused Owens of favoring the bill in order to advance his private banking fortune.[48] Near the end of the debate, Bristow wrote to Gilbert M. Hitchcock that the strong points "upon which we now stand are public ownership, government control, the rights of individual banks to have rediscounts, and the right of a regional bank to have currency upon demand."[49] But the midwestern senators could not hold together. Gradually, President Wilson forced the Democratic opposition into line, and on the final vote the Republican progressive forces split. Borah, Bristow, Clapp, and LaFollette voted against the bill, while Norris, Weeks, Poindexter, and Jones joined the Democrats to pass the Senate version of the Federal Reserve Act. In the joint conference committee Owen excluded the Republican members of the Banking and Currency Committee for fear that his fellow Democrats might join the Republicans against the measure.[50] Bristow could claim one partial victory, for Kansas City was made the headquarters for one reserve district.

Tension between President Wilson and the Republicans over the Federal Reserve Act did not abate, and when the President announced the selection of prominent businessmen and bankers to serve on the newly created board, the insurgents struck back. Senators Bristow and Nelson led a move to call two of Wilson's appointees, Paul M. Warburg and Thomas D. Jones, before the Banking and Currency Committee before their names were presented for confirmation to the Senate. Jones was a member of the "zinc trust" and a director of the International Harvester Company, which was under an antitrust indictment at the time. President Wilson defended his selection of Jones, claiming that as a member of the International Harvester Company he had tried to modify the practices of the company to conform to the new Clayton anti-trust law. But the committee hearings brought out facts contrary to Wilson's claim, and he withdrew Jones's nomination. F. A. Delano was nominated in Jones's place. Warburg, a partner in Kuhn, Loeb and Company and a competent authority on banking and currency, at first refused to appear before the Banking and Currency Committee, but President Wilson persuaded him to do so. The insurgents were unable to defeat Warburg and Delano. In fact, Bristow cast the only dissenting vote in the committee on Delano.[51]

The Warburg-Jones affair was more than a struggle for members of the Federal Reserve Board. Much like Taft, when Wilson was harassed by the insurgents he spoke out publicly against them. He claimed that the country was calling for a new temper in the affairs of politics and business and that the progressive antibusiness position was no longer popular. It was an ironical, but not necessarily related, fact that Senator Joseph L. Bristow was defeated in his bid for renomination to the Senate in the Kansas Republican primaries on the day that the Senate approved the nominations of Delano and Warburg. The editor of the New York *Times* pointed out that Bristow had been defeated by the reactionary Charles Curtis and suggested that Kansas electors had endorsed the claim of President Wilson that the turning point had come and that there was "need of a new temper toward business-men who have succeeded in business."[52]

Whether the temper of the country had changed is debatable, but it was clear that President Wilson was becoming more pro-business. The Warburg-Jones dispute was only one of many indications that the champion of the New Freedom was defending business interests. The long congressional struggle over the Clay-ton antitrust bill and the creation of a Federal Trade Commission brought out Wilson's lack of enthusiasm for dynamic restraints against malpractices of business. In their original forms both proposals had been weak, and much credit must be given to pro-gressives who helped strengthen the measures. Louis D. Brandeis' contribution to the drafting of a strong Federal Trade Commission Act cannot be overlooked, and the work of Senators Cummins, Clapp, and Bristow to strengthen this legislation was indeed effec-tive. Bristow and Clapp bitterly attacked the grave defects of the antitrust bill on October 2, 1914. Bristow characterized President Wilson as a tool of "sinister influences," declaring that no admin-istration in the last half-century had been so subservient to Wall Street.[53] Later the liberals protested against the weak appoint-ments Wilson made to the commission, pointing out the few gains made in regulating genuine business abuses. Undoubtedly they would have agreed with Brandeis, who in later years declared that "it was a stupid administration."[54]

Bristow engaged in many other activities during his two years under the Wilson administration. He supported the Smith-Lever bill which established a nationwide system of county agents.[55] He participated in the first vote in the Senate for his proposed constitutional amendment on woman suffrage. On July 22, 1913, Senator Benjamin R. Tillman of South Carolina inserted in the *Congressional Record* a violent attack on northern suffragettes, in the form of an article written by the Reverend Albert Taylor Bledsoe. Senators on both sides denounced the attack; Bristow called it an outrageous piece of "blackguardism." In response to the criticism, Tillman had the article stricken from the *Record*.[56] In his final days in the Senate, Bristow presented a bill to grant $1,000,000 to continue the 1912 irrigation study of the Great Plains. He urged the Department of Agriculture to back a $20,000,000 proposal for the construction of lakes and reservoirs in the plains area, emphasizing the need for harnessing the flood waters on the Arkansas and Platte rivers. Throughout these endeavors he argued that water was "more precious than gold."[57]

The newly created parcel post system had brought many problems. Bristow was chairman of a joint congressional committee to study the operation of the system, and he directed a thorough study of over thirty-seven thousand post offices. The committee studied cost, handling of packages, geographical areas using parcel post, the zone system, and rates. The study revealed extensive use of the system by the metropolitan areas of New York City and Chicago and the need for rates favoring the local commercial centers. Many recommendations were made for the improvement of the parcel post system, and this first study furnished a solid foundation upon which necessary changes in the postal system could be based.[58]

The influence of Bristow and his fellow progressives upon the Wilson administration is difficult to measure. The power of the progressives was weakened by their inability to stick together. Time and again Wilson was able to break what might have been a solid front, and it was easy for the public to conclude erroneously that the insurgents had opposed the Wilson administration for the mere sake of objecting. This disruption within the Republican party had a genuine impact on the election of 1914. The Democrats' lead in the House of Representatives was trimmed, and in several states the Republicans returned to power. But the return was to the conservative leadership within the Republican party. Joseph Bristow was a victim of this conservative swing. Charles Curtis defeated Bristow in the Republican primaries in 1914.

10

Defeat

Mark Sullivan, in 1912, told Albert Beveridge that the Progressive party was going to last because a great organizer and a rich man had, under the providence of God, been supplied to the party in the person of George W. Perkins.[1] But history was soon to prove that such a financial godfather could not make the Progressive party the leader in the United States.

A campaign slip for 1914, with crossed flags and a bull moose at the top, read:

> *Look up, not down*
> *Look out, not in*
> *Look forward, not backward*
> *And lend a hand.*[2]

The same slogan had been used in the Bull Moose campaign of 1912. But the defeat of Theodore Roosevelt in his campaign for the Presidency in 1912 had caused many liberals, especially elected politicians, to think over their positions again. At the national level Perkins and Roosevelt had kept up political pressure for an all-out victory in 1914. Roosevelt hoped to get the state leaders to make a third-party try again. If they won, all was well. If they lost, Roosevelt could still use their organization to press the old-guard Republicans to nominate him for the Presidency in 1916. Few of the state leaders perceived Roosevelt's strategy.

The liberals in the Republican party in Kansas had led since 1908, but the conservative forces were still powerful. The two elements in the party could make at best an uneasy truce, and popular dissatisfaction with the failure of Kansas legislators to accomplish economic reforms was growing. It seemed that now was the time to build a strong third-party organization within which the progressives from all backgrounds could unite to defeat the old guard in 1914. And William Allen White was the man to lead that organization. White had bucked the old-guard faction in his party for years; he was tired of intra-party wrangling. With the aid of David S. Hinshaw, a member of his newspaper staff who worked to set up an organization in each state, Dan Anthony, Governor Stubbs, Arthur Capper, Joseph Bristow, Henry Allen, Victor Murdock, and a group of state editors like M. M. Beck of the Holton *Recorder,* White hoped to form a third party and keep Kansas in the front lines of liberalism. For two years the building of the state organization was his chief interest.[3] In the beginning White was certain he needed the full support of Capper and Bristow, and he fought off all suggestions of fusionism.

It is easy to see why White took this position after 1912. The bulk of the correspondence in the White Papers reveals strong encouragement of his political efforts. Over and over, his correspondents urged him to continue the fight. A farmer from Holton wrote on December 9, 1912, "I will say that I certainly am not in favor of going back to the old Republican Party. I think it has outlived its usefulness." The writer suggested that there were many Democrats who thought that their party was progressive but these people could come into the new party.[4] An insurance agent from Kansas City wrote, "You can count on us for anything you want for the Progressive party. . . . We are in this fight to stay."[5] An evangelist pointed out the past failures of the Democratic party and predicted a speedy triumph for those citizens who had left the old party and taken their stand upon the "rights of man" rather than upon the "unseen foundation of the invisible government."[6] George W. Perkins wrote to White on November 13, 1912, that he felt certain "that it is worthwhile to continue the fight."[7] A professor of literature at Bethany College promised to do what he could to continue the movement because he believed in the "permanency of the cause."[8] Such was the spirit late in 1912, a spirit that was shown in many states.

Senator Joseph Bristow was fully aware of the battle lines that were being drawn. On November 9, 1912, he wrote to his son Frank: "Everything seems quite as usual, except politically there is a state of chaos, and no man's future is at all certain. I can see a hard fight ahead of me as the result of the political turmoil and the break-up of the Republican party. The popular animosity that has been engendered is greater than I have ever seen in my time. This is very largely between Republican factions."[9] On December 21, 1912, he wrote to Beveridge that he had much hesitation over the third party. He felt it might be best to run as an independent. "What is perplexing me now," wrote Bristow, "is the result if Wilson becomes an active progressive, standing for advanced ideas. Will he cut the ground from under us? Will he break up his own party, or will he cause the Democrats to go to the Republican party or organize a conservative Democratic party?" To Beveridge he expressed his belief that thousands had been drawn to progressivism because of their admiration for Theodore Roosevelt.[10] To his chief political adviser, John Harrison, he wrote, "I suppose there is no way to prevent the organization of a third party now. . . . but I want to follow my own course for a while."[11] On January 14, 1913, he wrote to his son Frank that it looked as though there would be three political parties in Kansas in two years—Republican, Democratic, and Progressive; "of course I will be the Progressive nominee, and hope to receive the nomination by acclamation."[12] About two weeks earlier he had confided to Beveridge that a reorganization of the parties into conservative and progressive was inevitable. It would be a matter of organization, as there were no doubts on principles.[13]

It was well known that Charles Curtis would make a bid for Republican support for Bristow's seat in the Senate. In his letters to Harrison, Bristow expressed his belief that he would have to turn to the Progressive ticket, but Harrison constantly cautioned him to delay.[14] Not announcing the party of his choice, early in February of 1913, Bristow sent U. S. Sartin a list of "What the Progressives Believe" to be read at a Kansas Progressive banquet. The list contained the main features of the Progressive platform of 1912 and emphasized placing judges under recall and adopting a plan by which the people could vote to retain a law, if the President and Congress agreed, even though the courts had declared it unconstitutional. It also called for an end to extortion by industrial tyranny.[15]

Throughout the spring and summer Bristow struggled with the problem of which party to identify himself with. He found three kinds of progressives in Kansas: Republican progressives who were for a third party, Republican progressives who would not leave the party, and Democratic progressives.[16] Many Republicans who had supported him would not leave the party. The enforced indecision made him very uncomfortable,[17] but his hesitancy was increased after a short trip in May to Michigan, where the Progressives were not advancing. He still toyed with the idea of running as an independent, and the standpatters were threatening his defeat even if they had to refuse to be bound by the primary election.

Meanwhile, White was building the third party and calling the harmony group "the cold toes brigade."[18] Beck wrote White that he felt both Bristow and Capper had blundered in not stating their position publicly and more emphatically.[19] He was encountering some opposition to a third party, opposition which he blithely ignored. E. W. Rankin wrote White that it was too little to endorse the direct election of senators, equal suffrage, and statewide primaries; the new party must reach forward to government ownership of railroads and telegraph and city ownership of utilities. These things were certain to come, and he was surprised that no party had taken up the "question of unequal interest rates."[20]

Bristow, meanwhile, was studying the actions of progressive Republicans in other states. Senator Cummins of Iowa was against the third-party movement, and his position no doubt influenced Bristow.[21] John Harrison still advised the Kansas senator to delay his announcement for re-election and to keep his enemies in the dark.[22] Early in November, Bristow wrote White that he was "not in complete accord" with Colonel Roosevelt and the direction the Progressive party had taken.[23] A few days later, in a bitter letter, he accused White of acting like a machine politician whose interest was solely in party organization and not issues. Bristow argued that while in the Senate he had supported all progressive measures regardless of party origin.[24] On November 29, 1913, he wrote former Senator Joseph Dixon that he thought the third party was going to evaporate.[25]

By this time it was clear that Bristow was not going into the third party. He was now convinced that a party progressive would have a hard time winning an election in Kansas. Frequently in his letters he mentioned the fifty thousand votes he would lose if he left the regular party. He wrote Henry Allen that he had talked with progressives who had supported him, and many had assured him that there was nothing to the Progressive party in Kansas except "Will White, Henry Allen and Stubbs." He declared to Allen that it would require far more courage to go into the Republican primary against Curtis and have White and the Kansas City *Star* fight him than to take the easy course and the Progressive nomination which would lead to defeat later.[26]

Bristow returned to Kansas for the Christmas holidays. On January 3, 1914, at 6 P.M. in Topeka, he announced that he would seek re-election on the Republican ticket, declaring that he had never been out of the party and that the idea of a third party was impractical. Bristow and his advisers had not foreseen the craftiness of "Will" White. Two hours after the Bristow announcement there came through the Associated Press, White's announcement that Victor Murdock would seek the nomination to the

United States Senate on the Progressive ticket. White had carefully timed his announcement so that it would appear in the same papers with Bristow's declaration.[27] In the words of David Hinshaw, White had "put mustard in Bristow's dishwater."[28]

White had clearly set the stage for a third party in Kansas and had passed the point of no return. He had turned against one of his best friends. Arthur Capper was soon to take a stand similar to Bristow's. When he did, White answered Capper with an announcement that Henry Allen would be the candidate for governor on the Progressive ticket. By his actions White had opened the door to victory for the conservative Charles Curtis. Votes that should have gone to Bristow would now go to Murdock, leaving Curtis a decided advantage in the party primary. White dramatically described the course of his action to Theodore Roosevelt on February 7, 1914. White declared that it would have been easy to return "Joe" to the Senate. But he felt that Bristow had gotten cold feet and that the Kansas senator wanted the progressives to "gently but firmly strangle" the Progressive party so that he could run as a Republican without opposition. This White could not do. Bristow had to declare himself a party progressive or "walk the plank."[29]

In a few days following his announcement Bristow sent out over five hundred letters to former supporters explaining that he was not deserting progressive principles. He believed he could do his best by staying within the Republican party. He described his decision as "the most disagreeable and hardest road he could have selected," but he believed he could do "more good and secure better results" in this way than in any other.[30]

The January political winds had struck Bristow with bonechilling force. Before the month had ended, former Senator Curtis had entered the race for the Senate and was bitterly denouncing Bristow and Capper for trying to make a deal to keep him out of the primary election. Standpat Republicans were giving Bristow the cold shoulder, and his former progressive friends were denouncing him as a traitor. "Will" White, his closest friend, was proclaiming that Bristow was guilty of a political felony.[31] Privately, Bristow was deeply hurt, but publicly he ignored White's malicious attacks and used the editorial pages of the Salina *Evening Journal* to state his case.[32]

A busy Senate schedule forced Bristow to hurry back to Washington. He elected, against the wishes of John Harrison and Roy Bailey, his political advisers, to remain in Washington until Congress was adjourned. He defended his decision on the grounds that "up to this time no Kansas Republican Senator in the history of Kansas has deserted his post of duty and made a personal campaign in behalf of his re-nomination."[33] But he found Wilson's continuous congressional sessions "disgusting" as they did not permit him to renew acquaintances with his constituents.[34]

Bristow's failure to return to Kansas left the success or failure of his primary campaign in the hands of his friends and a letter-writing staff in Washington. Harrison wrote Bristow that he was going to lose votes because of his opposition to Wilson's Mexican policy and the repeal of the Panama tolls.[35] On May 23, Bristow wrote to W. Y. Morgan that Capper, Akers, Davis, and Dawson thought that Curtis was gaining, and he urged Morgan to work on the newspapermen.[36]

Meanwhile, White proceeded to organize a state-wide Progressive party. One could question whether White read his mail, for by now many of his correspondents were against his treatment of Bristow. His actions were forcing friends of similar political opinions to take different sides.[37] White reported to Colonel Roosevelt on June 17 that he had completed the Progressive slate, but many of the candidates lacked enthusiasm; some would rather be defeated than elected. He saw in the Republican primary a life-and-death struggle between Curtis and Bristow, and he believed Curtis would win. If so, his victory would strengthen the Progressive ticket in the November election. In his own words, White had built a "splendid paper organization," but he did not know what it meant in votes.[38] On national issues White and his fellow Progressives were wishing upon a four-pointed star: government ownership of railroads, woman suffrage, national prohibition, and the economic and social demands of 1912 progressivism.[39] White served as chief treasurer and money-raiser in Kansas. George W. Perkins sent a personal check for five hundred dollars to aid Murdock.[40]

The third-party movement received a setback at both state and national levels when Roosevelt and Perkins endorsed Harvey D. Hinman as a fusion candidate for the governorship of New York. U. S. Sartin, chairman of the Kansas Progressive party, complained to White that this action "plays the Devil with the Progressive proposition in other states." He needled White about why Allen should not withdraw in favor of Capper, a good progressive, and Murdock, in favor of Bristow. Fusionism was proposed in Iowa and Nebraska. A row between Pinchot and Perkins increased the doubt about the outcome of the third party. Sartin insisted that Roosevelt and Perkins had wrecked the Progressive party in 75 per cent of the states.[41] In Bristow's opinion, the third party in his state was unfortunate and unjustifiable. Ardent Progressive idealists were misrepresenting and misstating the issues in a more ruthless manner than the earlier machine politicians.[42]

Hard times, especially in railroading and mining, and the failure of tariff reform to bring economic relief brought criticism upon the Bristow forces. Members of the typographical union led a strike against Bristow's own newspaper, and although he had resisted unionization before, this time he ordered Roy Bailey, his editor and manager, to recognize the union. He would lose too many votes if he opposed labor.[43] Bristow enlarged his Washington campaign staff and at one time had as many as fourteen workers sending out over three thousand letters a day. In one ten-day period he sent fifty thousand personal letters, distributed to all the counties.[44] Fay Seaton, Bristow's first secretary, had written a summary of Bristow's record in Congress, and some ninety thousand copies of the summary were mailed to Kansas voters. The state was flooded with Bristow's speeches; one hundred thousand copies of the speech on the tariff were printed, one hundred thousand on Panama tolls, twenty-five thousand on irrigation, and ten thousand on woman suffrage.[45] Bristow did not purchase advertising in the local presses. In June he wrote to his son Frank that he had not been sending him any money lately "because I have been needing all I have here, conducting a pretty expensive" campaign. He was certain that if Mrs. Bristow knew how much he was spending she would "kick about it." She was not anxious to have him return to Washington, although she did not wish to see him beaten by the men who had elected him.[46]

The session of Congress lasted beyond the time of the primary election in Kansas, and Bristow's absence from the state was a decided advantage for his opponent. Curtis was a hard and effective campaigner. He worked for the old soldier vote, the suffragettes, and the city vote. Over and over he accused Bristow of growing away from the people in the state. He argued that Bristow did not care about the people—if he cared for Kansans, why was he not at home campaigning?[47]

In spite of Curtis' apparent gains Bristow believed he might win by 25,000 votes.[48] On the evening of the primary election, the Bristows entertained the Senator's staff and friends from Kansas in their Virginia home. What started as a joyous evening soon lengthened uncomfortably. No telegrams came from home, and the party waited long into the night for congratulatory wires. Gradually the Senator realized that the absence of telegrams meant that he had failed in his bid for renomination. He was stunned.[49] The decision was not final even on August 5, but by August 6 the news stories gave the victory to Curtis.[50] Curtis had won 44,612 votes to Bristow's 42,772. Two minor Republican contestants had entered the primary: Henry F. Tucher polled 20,237 votes and A. M. Henry 6,060. Curtis' lead in Shawnee and Leavenworth counties was sufficient to defeat Bristow, although Bristow had carried sixty-two counties to Curtis' forty-three. Murdock, the Progressive, had drawn only 12,716 votes, and there was little hope that the third party could succeed in November. White, by his break with Bristow, had guaranteed a return of Republican conservatives in Kansas.

On August 6, Bristow wrote to M. F. Amrine: "It was too bad the progressives had to divide up and let the reactionaries come into control of the government. I have done everything I could to prevent it. This third party movement is a failure." He continued in a philosophical vein, "But that is the history of all great reform movements, and those of us who go into the fight must expect to be sacrificed in the end by the inconsistency of the excessive ardor of many of our supporters."[51] On the same day he wrote to Capper, "I regret to lose, but I have the satisfaction of having done what I thought was the right thing and served my state during my term with faithfulness."[52]

In most of his post-campaign letters, Bristow was bitter toward White, feeling that Allen had run against his better judgment. He wrote that Capper could have worked harder for him through the *Capital* and that Dan Anthony had given little aid in northeastern Kansas. "Billy" Morgan was the "best worker in the field." At one time he sadly questioned the use of the primary which he had earlier sustained.[53] But by mid-August he felt the greatest error was that he had not returned to campaign in June and July.[54] By this time he was ready to return to Kansas at the close of the congressional session and join in the fall campaign, and he pledged himself to aid Arthur Capper in his try for the governorship. He returned to his home late in October. In four days he made nineteen speeches in six of the eight congressional districts.

The results of the November election were disastrous to the Progressives in Kansas and the nation. As Bristow described the defeat to Fred C. Trigg, on November 6, 1914, "In the nation, this campaign has resulted in sending Roosevelt to the scrap pile and in Kansas it has resulted in the retirement from public life of every leader that has any progressive tendencies."[55]

Bristow returned to Washington for the short session of Congress. At home Roy Bailey tried to pick up the political pieces, seeking assistance from White, Capper, and others to arrange Bristow's appointment to the Kansas Public Utilities Commission.[56] The editor of the New York *Sun,* on March 6, 1915, described Bristow's departure from Washington. He declared that the Senate would lose a "picturesque figure . . . the most aggressive of the band of progressives." Bristow had qualities that everyone thought would return him to the Senate, but, according to the editor, he was defeated by a "reactionary." The press soon announced that Governor Arthur Capper of Kansas had appointed the retiring senator to the Public Utilities Commission. Kansas had not completely lost Bristow's public service, but she no longer had a thorough, hard-working liberal representing her in the United States Senate.

The Long Years

When Joseph L. Bristow left the Senate, he could have remained free from public service, either returning to Kansas as editor of the Salina *Evening Journal* or remaining on the farm that he had purchased on the Virginia side of the Potomac. By 1915 the *Journal* was making a good return on his investment, largely because of skillful management by Roy Bailey, who had taken over as manager and editor in 1911. Bailey had served as a cub reporter for William Allen White and Henry Allen. After he joined the *Journal,* Bristow sold him a $4,000 share in the paper, which he paid for at the rate of $10 per week, and soon he removed a debt of $15,000 for the *Journal.*[1] In November, 1914, Bristow incorporated the Journal Publishing Company for $50,000; the shares cost $100 each and Bristow, Bailey, Frank Bristow, George M. Hull, and Hazel Schuee were the principal shareholders.[2]

The new incorporation brought satisfactory results. On January 22, 1917, Bristow wrote to Aubrey Harwell of the New York *Times* that the *Journal* had been a leading newspaper in Salina for over twenty-five years: "It is established, has the prestige which age and success give it and is paying me an annual income of 6 per cent or more on $100,000. During the last ten years it has doubled in value every five years, and I have not the slightest doubt that it will double in value again within the next ten years."[3] The corporation continued until 1925. On December 2, 1925, Roy Bailey and R. J. Loubengayer became the new owners of the Journal Publishing Company.[4] Bailey worked with the *Journal* for thirty-eight years, and, in addition, he bought and sold other Kansas papers during that time.

Bristow's second choice could have been to settle down on the Virginia farm, known as Ossian Hall, that he had purchased in 1914. In an enthusiastic letter to his son Frank on August 7, 1914, Bristow wrote that he had purchased the six-hundred-acre farm and, "The house sits in the finest grove I have seen in Virginia."[5] He described the five-acre yard and the fifteen or twenty varieties of forest trees that surrounded the stately mansion. Ten-room Ossian Hall had been owned at the time of the Revolutionary War by Dr. Richard Stewart, a son-in-law of Martha Washington. It was said to have been built in 1732 by the men who built Mt. Vernon, and was restored in 1912–13.

The farm lay along the Accotink Run for about a mile. Across the road was Ravensworth, a Fitzhugh estate, owned in 1914 by Colonel Robert E. Lee, a grandson of General Robert E. Lee. The farm was twelve miles from the District of Columbia, one and a half miles from the Springfield station, and a half-mile from Annandale. There were four cold springs that ran even on a dry August day, and from them came beautiful running brooks. There were 350 acres of timber which he estimated would yield from $12,000 to $18,000 in lumber. He planned to sell his home in the District and his farm land in Salina to finance the new farm. In April, 1915, he wrote that he would live half of the time in Virginia and the other half in Kansas and incidentally make plans for another campaign.[6] Later, Bristow added two large farms from Frye and Lee lands in order to connect with the Little River Pike. These last purchases increased his holdings to four thousand three hundred acres.

Bristow set to work with enthusiasm and keen agricultural sense to develop his new holdings. He and Colonel Lee persuaded the Fairfax County board of supervisors to develop private roads to their homes. Bristow's youngest son, Ed, moved to the farm, and with four helpers the father and son set out to rebuild the land. They spread lime on the soil, built woven-wire fences, set up a sawmill, and experimented with farm tractors. Soon there were four hundred acres of good pasture stocked with Red Polled cattle and Dorset sheep. Bristow enjoyed riding a fine roan mare he had bought and took pride in the ribbons his produce and animals won at the Fairfax County fair in 1915. He wrote that the people at the fair were surprised at the quality of corn grown on the old farm. Bristow's close friend, Senator Moses Clapp, had purchased land in Maryland, and the two gentlemen farmers exchanged many letters on their agricultural interests. At one time Bristow evaluated his new estate at $50,000.[7]

In 1927, two years after Bristow sold the *Journal,* the editor of *Time* magazine described the "old irreconcilable" as a man surrounded by silos and shrubbery. Bristow had subdivided some of the farm and was selling city lots. The editor wrote that Bristow was now a peaceable country gentleman with only a "LaFollette Avenue" running through his subdivision to recall a stirring past.[8] Roy Bailey tells the story that Bristow was showing some of his Kansas friends the new lots at Annandale, and some one remarked that the lot set aside for a bank carried quite a high price. Henry Allen asked Bristow what he would do with the *unearned increment.* Bristow, the foe of *unearned increment* in his progressive days, with a red face replied, "I am going to keep it."[9] By 1937 the Topeka *Capital* described Bristow as one of the most successful farmers in Virginia, "a gentleman farmer in the best sense of the term." Bristow was still loyal to Kansas, returning every year to the state to vote and to attend the meeting of the trustees of Baker University.[10]

At the close of his Senate career, Bristow did not choose to retire from public life. In January, 1914, when Bristow and Arthur Capper had decided to remain in the Republican party,

Capper had assured Bristow of a state appointment if the latter were defeated in the primary election. This promise, of course, was contingent on Capper's being elected governor. Soon after Capper's victory, William Allen White started a campaign to make Bristow chairman of the Kansas Public Utilities Commission. He contacted many former Bull Moosers, urging them to encourage Bristow to accept and claiming that this appointment would "spell out as nothing else would" Capper's determination to be as progressive as his party "would let him." It would give Bristow a position in Kansas politics from which his ideas and conception of political duty would be impressed upon the state and keep alive "progressive things," and it would give to the people of Kansas "a quality of ability and intelligence" never before displayed on the Public Utilities Commission. The appointment would also keep Bristow's name before the people during the next four years.[11]

Bristow advised the Governor to look elsewhere when the invitation was made. He felt it would be inadvisable to accept the offer, partly because it would be a financial sacrifice and he needed a year's rest. Furthermore, he did not want to be a chronic office seeker.[12] Bristow's friends pressed him to take the position, however, and he accepted Capper's offer on December 16, 1914. He assumed his duties on April 1, 1915, assuring his family and friends that he would take the work "deliberately."[13] Such a promise had a hollow ring, for Joe Bristow was never inclined to conserve his energy. He entered on his new tasks in a period when pressures were at a new height.

Many midwestern railroads had lost money in 1914, and before Bristow joined the Kansas Utilities Commission, they had requested permission from the Interstate Commerce Commission to increase freight and passenger rates. The Kansas commission had joined those of seven other states in making plans to appear before the I.C.C. to check these requested increases. Meanwhile, thirteen roads had petitioned the Kansas commission to increase the two-cent passenger fare to three cents a mile, and these requests soon went before the I.C.C.[14] At this time in the Midwest, most state utility commissions, in accordance with the ideals of the progressive movement, were trying to keep railroad rates as low as possible. The big railroads, feeling safer under the supervision of the I.C.C., were making a concerted drive to free themselves from state control.

The Kansas commission studied the accident rate of the railroad companies and the need for better roadbeds and more safety devices, as well as attempting to make a scientific evaluation of all of the public utilities for tax purposes. Another activity that took a large share of the commission's time was the consolidation of telephone companies. Once a consolidation was made, there was usually a petition for an increase in telephone rates. In a normal two-year period the commission made as many as one thousand decisions concerning such rate increases.

By April 7, Bristow was in the midst of local rate hearings, and he toured the state with members of the tax commission to study the assessed value of public utilities. In the same month he appeared before the I.C.C. in Chicago. In May he spent ten days in Washington attempting to work out a formula with the I.C.C. on decisions concerning interstate and state business. In July he added a statistician to his staff and began the preparation of his brief for the appearance of the eight midwestern states before the I.C.C. to discuss railroad rates. After making his usual thorough search for facts, he sent copies of his brief to Borah, Clapp, Cummins, LaFollette, Kenyon, and Norris. He worked for over two years on the case before the I.C.C. Some of Bristow's eastern friends suggested that investments in public service corporations in Kansas would not be very desirable while Joe was at the head of the Kansas commission.[15]

Bristow used the Kansas City and Southern as a test case on the evaluation of a road, and studies showed that the railroads frequently ascribed too high a proportion of their costs to passenger service. The Kansas Utilities Commission tried to separate expenses for freight and passenger service and eventually decided upon the gross-ton mile as a measuring stick for costs of roads.[16] The commission was firm in its denial of increases, saving its citizens over $2,000,000 a year during the delay.[17] And delay it was. Injunctions and court rulings all took time. It was not until January, 1918, that the Supreme Court upheld retention of the two-cent fare for Illinois, in a case in which Kansas had been a partner.[18] Even then the victory was short-lived. In May and June of 1918, William G. McAdoo, the wartime director-general for the nation's railroads, granted the three-cent passenger rate and an increase in freight rates. The Topeka *Journal* estimated that the McAdoo decision would cost Kansans $27,500,000 a year.[19] The Kansas commission had approved some increases in rates before the McAdoo ruling, but it had been able to protect state lines and had kept a tight reign on the roads during the war.

In 1915, Bristow was made chairman of the legislative committee for the National Association of Railway Commissioners. In that capacity he joined the fight to save state control of the local railroads. In January, 1918, he appeared before a Senate committee to protest the passage of a bill authorizing the director-general to supersede state commissions. He was gratified to find a majority of the committee at that time favored protecting the interest of the states.[20]

Bristow wrote the *Third Biennial Report* for the Kansas Public Utilities Commission. This 610-page report reflected the trials and tribulations of a young and pioneering commission. Commissioner Bristow traced the excellent growth of the several departments that carried on the work of the commission, and he described fully the diverse and varied cases that had required decisions by the commission. Several recommendations were made to the state legislature to make the commission more effective. A reasonable fee was requested from all companies issuing stocks and bonds. There was need for a better codification of the Utilities Act of 1911, and the commission's position before the courts needed to be clarified. Automobile accidents at railroad crossings had brought a high death toll, and the commission recommended overhead or undergrade crossings for heavy traffic areas. Dealing with some eighteen hundred telephone companies in Kansas led the commission to seek power to force telephone companies to connect services. There was need for uniform methods of stringing wires over highways and public roads. The commission also sought to legalize the right of appeal by individuals and companies from rulings by city councils and commissions.[21]

Bristow assisted in writing the fourth report of the commission, but resigned from his job before the report was completed. Problems connected with telephone companies had eased, but the high death rate in rail and auto accidents still worried the commission. One of the strongest recommendations of this report was the need to prevent duplication of services by utility firms in the same community.

While serving on the commission, Bristow kept up his extensive correspondence with political leaders, made public speeches, and wrote articles on current political issues. Early in 1915 he joined the liberals who were urging the nomination of A. B. Cummins of Iowa as a Republican presidential candidate in 1916. Cummins had won 40,257 votes in the Iowa Republican primary out of a total of 45,382 votes. Iowa supporters of Theodore Roosevelt had garnered only 2,384 votes.[22] Bristow wanted a more militant candidate, but he sensed a lack of sentiment for LaFollette or anyone of a radical tendency. Cummins' nomination might draw the Bull Moosers back to the regular party.[23] Bristow described the Iowa leader as an honest, conscientious, sincere, and thorough progressive. He knew that Cummins lacked the political genius of Roosevelt and the phrase-making skill of Wilson, but he concluded that Cummins would make the best President.[24]

Kansas Republicans backed Roosevelt at first, but later swung to Cummins. Bristow's efforts were not too effective, for the Curtis crowd had kept him from attending the national convention as a delegate.[25] He likened the lethargy in Republican Kansas to the atmosphere during the election in 1892,[26] and he recognized the power of the conservative Republicans on the national level. He believed that the standpatters would nominate Elihu Root if they dared, but otherwise they would turn to Charles Evans Hughes. Bristow wrote that "with the Barnes-Wadsworth-Crane-Penrose crowd it is anything to beat Roosevelt," and they decided that Hughes would be "the most durable," if they could not promote one of their own safely.[27] Bristow supported Hughes, but he campaigned very little. He turned down LaFollette's invitation to campaign in Wisconsin, but he did spend ten days on the campaign circuit in his home state during the closing days of the campaign.[28] He confided to friends that he was disappointed over the results in Kansas.

Although Bristow's campaign efforts were slight in 1916, he planned to recapture a seat in the United States Senate in 1918. A successful record on the Public Utilities Commission, supported by a favorable press, would no doubt enhance his chances for re-election in 1918. Unfortunately, World War I changed the picture. Bristow's critical attitude toward President Wilson's conduct of the war and his violent attacks on war profiteering lost him political support by 1918.

As a public-spirited citizen, Bristow observed the outbreak of World War I in Europe. His letters reflect his thoughts on the causes of the war and his hopes for a permanent peace. Like many Americans he had a deep distrust of monarchical forms of government, and he declared that this "utterly unnecessary" war was the result of the ambitions of the reigning monarchs of Europe. He believed that the war would not have occurred if Germany, Russia, and Austria had had popular governments. Throughout his letters he was unsympathetic to the idea that huge armies and power promoted peace. At the same time he regarded the prohibition of the export of arms as a very superficial way to promote peace propaganda. He saw disarmament as a certain road to peace. If the war could overthrow the reigning monarchs of Europe, disarmament would be easy. Unless the European war destroyed the German military system, the war would be "an utter failure."[29]

In May, 1915, the editor of the New York *Times* wired Bristow for a statement on the sinking of the *Lusitania*. Bristow replied that the sinking was "a crime more infamous than piracy and [it] should be so treated by the governments of all civilized nations."[30] The gains of Germany through submarine power worried Bristow, and by July, 1915, he wrote that the war in Europe had demonstrated the American need for a good submarine fleet to prevent the combined nations of Europe from invading the United States.[31]

Once the United States entered World War I, it was not the fear of submarines, but the fear of the dulling of the American conscience that bothered Bristow. Through his public speeches, interviews, and the columns of the *Evening Journal,* he bitterly attacked President Wilson's conduct of the war. With the "old progressive zeal" he criticized the abandonment of the volunteer system, the high cost of the construction of new military camps, the excessive profits allowed by the government, the release of companies from antitrust laws, the seekers of "safe" jobs far from the firing line, and many other apparent excesses brought on by entry into the war.[32] He wrote Senator Borah that he had gotten into the "bitterest controversy" he had ever had in his life through some of his attacks on the Wilson administration: He was being denounced as a traitor by the pro-Wilson followers and held as a self-sacrificing patriot by those who agreed with him. He had no hesitation about the justice of his criticisms. He granted that there might be some question of expediency, but he had "no doubt" that ultimately every criticism he had made would be approved overwhelmingly.[33] In a public letter to Representative Guy T. Helvering, he summarized his criticisms and concluded:

> You may think it patriotic to draw the youth of this land to die in the trenches of Europe and to permit the bloated munition maker to escape proper taxation and keep his blood-stained gold—*but we do not.* And regardless of the brazen effrontery with which you seek to intimidate men from the expression of the facts, we propose to continue to portray the conditions as they are, not as a traitor to his country but as a patriot who has contempt for a Congressional trimmer and hatred for a public thief.[34]

Bristow's opposition to Wilson's direction of the war continued. Many Republicans felt that he was too extreme in his criticism. His paper in Salina lost advertisers. His position was similar to that of Robert LaFollette, whose opposition to wartime policies led to the accusation that he was pro-German.

On January 16, 1917, Bristow wrote to White that Governor Capper had understood "all along that I would be a candidate for the Senate," but now Capper was seeking advice from Bristow's friends on the question of his own candidacy for the Senate.[35] Bristow left the Utilities Commission in March of 1918 and began his formal campaign in April. Three other vote-getting Kansas Republicans, Capper, Stubbs, and Charles Scott, filed for the primary. Hostility to Bristow was best shown at Ellsworth, where Democratic leaders denied him the use of the city hall. Later when he was denied the use of the city hall at Norton, Bristow stood on a chair in front of the Norton *Times* office and delivered his campaign speech.[36]

The outcome of the August primary was a major defeat for former Senator Bristow. Capper polled 103,120 votes, Stubbs 31,614, Scott 24,286, and Bristow 13,911. Clearly, Bristow's political life was ended in Kansas. But he gallantly declared that it was too late to complain. He had now paid the full penalty for pioneering as a progressive.[37] Years later, in an interview with Fola LaFollette, he said he got the worst beating of his life, but he still insisted that if he had to do it over again he would follow the same course.[38] After his defeat Bristow campaigned for the Republican party, and for a time he remained in Kansas, speaking on the Chautauqua platform and at other public meetings. He and the family returned for good to Ossian Hall in 1922. From there he advised other politicians that the best way to retire from politics was to "buy a farm and be happy."[39]

Ossian Hall became an object of pilgrimage for many of the old-time progressives, as well as younger men who frequently sought Bristow's advice. He worked hard, kept up his correspondence, and read history and political science extensively. But life at Ossian Hall was not always easy. On April 23, 1932, Mrs. Bristow died. Three years later on March 30, 1935, his youngest son died. Bristow helped to rear seven orphaned grandchildren.

On June 16, 1944, Bristow fell on the street. He died at 2:00 A.M., July 14, 1944. In the press and in private letters, hundreds of people paid tribute to the former senator from Kansas. Many recalled his courageous political leadership as an insurgent: Throughout his long years of service, he had never lost his faith in progressivism. A most fitting tribute was published in 1960 by John Walton who wrote that "whether on the farm or in the Senate, Joseph L. Bristow was surrounded by an unmistakable aura of greatness."[40]

Notes

CHAPTER I

1. New York *Daily Tribune,* Jan. 22, 1861.
2. See Kentucky list of Union soldiers in Kentucky Historical Society, Frankfort. According to it, William Bristow was wounded at Piketon, Kentucky, November, 1861.
3. Biographical sketch of Joseph Little Bristow, Bristow Papers, Archives Division, Kansas State Historical Society, Topeka. The various spellings of the family name make tracing records difficult. Joseph's father, William, spelled his name "Bristo" on his enlistment in the Union army. One also finds "Bristoe," as well as "Bristow," in family records.
4. For material on William Bristow see Hazel Green (Ky.) *Herald,* May 13, 1897; biographical sketch, Bristow Papers; Joseph L. Bristow, *Fraud in Politics at the Turn of the Century,* eds. Joseph Q. and Frank B. Bristow (New York, 1952); Frank W. Blackmar, *Kansas—A Cyclopedia of State History* (Chicago, 1912), Part I, 371-72; William E. Connelley, *A Standard History of Kansas and Kansans* (Topeka, 1918), III, 1255-57; Blackmar, pp. 391-92, reviews William's military career.
5. Children born to William and his second wife were John, William, Bertha, and Hattie.
6. Interview by James B. Murrow in St. Louis *Globe Democrat,* Mar. 20, 1909, reproduced in Salina *Evening Journal,* Mar. 25, 1909.
7. *Ibid.*
8. *Ibid.*
9. Homer K. Ebright, *History of Baker University* (Baldwin, Kans., 1951), pp. 101 ff.; W. H. Sweet, *Fourteen Years of My Life* (a pamphlet published probably in 1886), a copy in Baker University Library, Baldwin, Kans.
10. Ebright, *History of Baker University,* p. 109.
11. Baldwin *Index,* Jan. 1886, p. 14.
12. Baldwin *Ledger,* Apr. 15, 1885.
13. *Ibid.,* July 31, 1885. This rapid change in ownership reminds one of the comment of J. S. Gilmore in the Neodosha *Weekly Citizen,* February 2, 1872, that "the Oswego *Republican* has appeared for four weeks in succession without changing hands."
14. Salina *Evening Journal,* Mar. 25, 1909.
15. Frank C. Lockwood, "Senator Bristow from Kansas," *The Outlook,* XC (Nov. 21, 1908) 617-19.
16. Bristow to R. N. Allen, Mar. 8, 1909, Bristow Papers.
17. Bristow said he received the advice from a former Union veteran, Colonel Buckner. Salina *Evening Journal,* Mar. 25, 1909.
18. Baldwin *Ledger,* Nov. 6, 1886.
19. The *Alumni Record* of Baker University (1st ed., 1917), p. 76, lists the Bristow children: William H., born Oct. 19, 1880; Bertha M., Dec. 18, 1881; Joseph Q., Mar. 5, 1884; Frank B., Dec. 13, 1885; Edwin M., Feb. 18, 1888. William and Bertha died in infancy.
20. Lawrence *Journal,* Sept. 22, 1890.
21. Kirke Mechem, ed., *The Annals of Kansas* (Topeka, 1954), I (1886-1910), 110.
22. *Ibid.,* I, 135-36.
23. *Ibid.,* I, 146-49.
24. *Ibid.,* I, 181.
25. Georgia, Alabama, North Carolina, South Carolina, Tennessee, Nebraska, Colorado, and Wyoming. Salina *Daily Republican,* Mar. 1, 1894.
26. *Ibid.*
27. *Ibid.,* Apr. 14, 1894.

28. *Ibid.,* Mar. 9, May 28, 1894.
29. *Ibid.,* July 2, 1894; Topeka *Capital,* June 26, 1894: "Bristow is a busy man and a great worker, but he is arranging his business so as to devote most of his time to the work of the committee during the campaign."
30. Topeka *Capital,* Oct. 3–5, 1894. McKinley had spoken in Leavenworth in 1892.
31. A partial roll call would include:

Morton Albaugh, editor of the Kingman *Leader Courier;* D. R. Anthony, Leavenworth *Times;* William Allen White, Emporia *Gazette;* Fred C. Trigg, who moved from Bristow's Salina paper to the Kansas City *Star;* Charles F. Scott, Iola *Register;* Henry Allen, Ottawa *Herald* and Wichita *Beacon;* W. Y. Morgan, Hutchinson *News;* Victor Murdock, Wichita *Eagle;* and Arthur Capper, Topeka *Capital.*

CHAPTER II

1. *Irrigation Farmer,* Feb., 1894. (Citations for the *Irrigation Farmer* will be for the month in which the issue appeared. The publisher seldom used page numbers in the journal.)
2. Lawrence *Journal,* May 18, 1894, reproduced in Salina *Daily Republican,* May 25, 1894.
3. *Ibid.*
4. *Irrigation Age,* VI (Feb., 1894), 75.
5. *Ibid.,* VI, 158; *Irrigation Farmer,* Apr., 1894; Salina *Daily Republican,* Mar. 23, 24, 1894.
6. *Irrigation Farmer,* Sept., 1894.
7. *Ibid.,* Oct. and Nov., 1894; see Garden City *Herald,* Oct. 6, 1894, for a description of the pumping displays.
8. Salina *Daily Republican,* May 25, 1894.
9. *Irrigation Farmer,* Mar., 1895.
10. *Ibid.,* July, 1894.
11. *Ibid.,* Mar., 1895; *Sixth Biennial Report of the Commission of Forestry and Irrigation for the Period Ending June 30, 1898* (Topeka, 1898), pp. 77 ff.
12. *Report of the Kansas Board of Irrigation Survey and Experiment, 1895–1896, to the Legislature of Kansas* (Topeka, 1897), pp. 206–10.
13. State of Kansas, *Session Laws of 1895* (Topeka, 1895), Chap. 162, 300–305.

14. D. M. Frost was president of the Kansas State Irrigation Association; Sutton was president of the State Board of Agriculture and president of the Sixth Congressional District Irrigation Association; Tomblin was a Populist member and a large landowner and irrigator in Sherman County. H. V. Hinckley was appointed engineer. *Irrigation Farmer,* Mar., 1895.
15. Wells were sunk in the following counties: Hamilton, Gray, Grant, Sherman, Logan, Wichita, Greeley, Lane, Haskell, Trego, Rawlins, Rooks, Ford, Seward, Sheridan, Hodgeman, and Wallace.
16. For details of the experiments from 1895 to 1896 see *Report of the Kansas Board of Irrigation Survey and Experiment, 1895–1896, to the Legislature of Kansas.* On page 10 the board summarized its work; on pp. 146 ff. are several scholarly reports. The *Irrigation Farmer* from March to October, 1895, carried detailed accounts of the work of the board.
17. State of Kansas, *Session Laws of 1897,* Chap. 21, 52–53.
18. *Department of Forestry and Irrigation, State of Kansas,* Bulletin No. 1 (Topeka, 1898). See especially pp. 4–11 and 25–27.

CHAPTER III

1. William F. Zornow, *Kansas: A History of the Jayhawk State* (Norman, Okla., 1957), pp. 203–205.

2. Troy *Chief*, Sept. 26, 1895; Topeka *State Journal*, Apr. 25, 1895, June 26, 1896; William A. White, *Autobiography of William Allen White* (New York, 1946), pp. 273, 304–18.

3. Topeka *Capital*, July 3, Aug. 12, Sept. 15, 1896.

4. Ottawa *Herald*, Nov. 5, 1896.

5. John D. Bright, ed., *Kansas: The First Century* (New York, 1956), I, 485; Zornow, *Kansas*, pp. 203–205.

6. Joseph L. Bristow, *Fraud in Politics at the Turn of the Century*, eds. Joseph Q. and Frank B. Bristow (New York, 1952), pp. 22–27. The manuscript for this book was found among Bristow's papers by his sons. It was possibly prepared by Bristow as a memoir of his work in the postal service from 1897–1905.

7. *Ibid.*, pp. 27–31.

8. Topeka *Capital*, Mar. 12, 14, 1897.

9. *Ibid.*, Mar. 18, 19, 1897.

10. *Ibid.*, Mar. 21, 1897.

11. Kansas City *Star*, Mar. 22, 1897.

12. Margaret Leech, *In the Days of McKinley* (New York, 1959), pp. 105–10. Dorothy G. Fowler, *The Cabinet Politician: The Postmasters General 1829–1909* (New York, 1943), pp. 246–61. See McKinley to Hanna, Feb. 12 and Feb. 18, 1897, McKinley Papers, Division of Manuscripts, Library of Congress, Washington; Herbert David Croly, *Marcus Alonzo Hanna* (New York, 1912), pp. 231–33; Charles G. Dawes, *A Journal of the McKinley Years* (New York, 1950), pp. 250–51.

13. Leech, *In the Days of McKinley*, p. 285; Fowler, *The Cabinet Politician*, pp. 250–51.

14. *Ibid.*, pp. 263-64, 286; A. Bower

Sageser, *First Two Decades of the Pendleton Act* (Lincoln, Nebr., 1935), p. 230.

15. Bristow, *Fraud in Politics*, pp. 31–40; Fowler, *The Cabinet Politician*, p. 252.

16. Bristow, *Fraud in Politics*, Appendix B., p. 116.

17. *Ibid.*, p. 34; Sageser, *First Two Decades of the Pendleton Act*, pp. 206–207.

18. Bristow, *Fraud in Politics*, pp. 34 ff. McKinley's administration established the system of referees.

19. *Ibid.*, pp. 41–51.

20. *Ibid.*, pp. 48–51.

21. *Annual Reports of the Post Office Department for the Fiscal Year Ending June 30, 1898* (Washington, D.C.), pp. 835–74. (Hereafter cited as Post Office Department, *Annual Reports*.)

22. Post Office Department, *Annual Reports*, 1905, pp. 661–79.

23. For the work of the postal inspectors see the *Annual Reports* for 1900–1902.

24. United States Civil Service Commission, *Fifteenth Report* (1897–1898), p. 20; Sageser, *First Two Decades of the Pendleton Act*, pp. 214–17.

25. *Ibid.*, pp. 218–20; Leech, *In the Days of McKinley*, pp. 471–72; Fowler, *The Cabinet Politician*, pp. 254–55; *Good Government*, Vol. VII, July 15, 1899. The National Civil Service Reform Association, on June 5, 1899, declared that it was a backward step.

26. Fowler, *The Cabinet Politician*, pp. 255–60; Sageser, *First Two Decades of the Pendleton Act*, pp. 216–17; *Good Government*, Vol. VIII, May 15, 1900, February 15, 1901.

27. Bristow, *Fraud in Politics*, pp. 96–100; Leech, *In the Days of McKinley*, p. 534.

28. Bristow, *Fraud in Politics*, pp. 100–101; Topeka *State Journal*, June 29, 1900; Robert M. La-

Follette, *Autobiography,* (Madison, Wisc., 1913), pp. 131–33. In 1913, Bristow wrote a memo for LaFollette on his interview with McKinley. LaFollette used most of the memo in his account. See Bristow Papers, Archives Division of Kansas State Historical Society, Topeka.

29. United States Senate Committee on Relations with Cuba, *Criticism of E. G. Rathbone on the Bristow Report . . . December 12, 1900.*

30. Reeves was pardoned by Governor General Wood because he was a witness. When Cuba became a republic, Neely was granted amnesty. At first Rathbone refused amnesty under $100,000 bond. After a three-year fight, aided by Hanna's financial support, Rathbone won amnesty from the Cuban government. New York *Tribune,* June 24, 1902, Mar. 23, 1903, Aug. 25, 1903.

31. Undated memorandum on the work of Harrison in the Bristow Papers.

32. Post Office Department, *Annual Reports,* 1900, pp. 17–21.

33. Dawes, *A Journal of the McKinley Years,* p. 240.

34. Because of his successful handling of later postal frauds, Bristow was suggested in 1903 as a vice-presidential candidate. New York *Times,* June 21, 1903; Topeka *Journal,* June 22, 1903.

35. For the attitude of the reformers see William D. Foulke, *Fighting the Spoilsmen* (New York, 1919), pp. 55–56; Frederic Bancroft, ed., *Speeches and Correspondence of Carl Schurz* (New York, 1913), VI, 381; *Harper's Weekly,* XLV (Dec. 28, 1901), 1326.

36. Payne to Theodore Roosevelt, Aug. 7, 1903, Roosevelt Papers, Division of Manuscripts, Library of Congress, Washington.

37. Bonaparte to L. B. Swift, Oct. 31, 1904, Bonaparte Papers, Division of Manuscripts, Library of Congress, Washington. For an evaluation of Roosevelt's record on civil service see Sageser, *First Two Decades of the Pendleton Act,* pp. 224–40 and Fowler, *The Cabinet Politician,* pp. 266–71.

38. *Investigation of the Post Office Department* 1903–1904, 58th Cong., 2nd sess., *Senate Doc., Nos. 151–81,* V, 5–6, contains a review of the early facts in a memorandum submitted by President Roosevelt to Congress.

39. Roosevelt to Payne, Apr. 27, 1903, Roosevelt Papers. See Washington *Post,* Mar. 29, Apr. 1–8, 1903. On April 12 the *Post* declared the scandals were as bad as the star route frauds.

40. White expressed this idea to Lodge on May 28, 1903, and Lodge sent it on to Roosevelt, June 2, 1903. Roosevelt Papers.

41. Washington *Post,* Apr. 24, 1903. Charges of safe rifling were brought against Mrs. Tyner.

42. Bristow to Payne, May 7, 1903, copy in Roosevelt Papers. Washington *Post,* May 9, 1903. Fosner had served with Bristow in the Cuban investigation.

43. Lodge to Roosevelt, May 20, 1903, Roosevelt Papers; New York *Tribune,* June 19, 1903.

44. Payne to Roosevelt, June 27, 1903, Roosevelt Papers. Payne had given orders to the staff not to give out stories without consent of the head of the department.

45. Lodge to Roosevelt, May 30, 1903, Roosevelt Papers.

46. Bristow to Payne, Aug. 20, 1903, copies in the Roosevelt Papers.

47. Post Office Department Letter Books, Nos. 56–58, National Archives, Washington.

48. Lodge to Roosevelt, June 27, 1903, Roosevelt Papers. Lodge was unhappy over the selection of Bonaparte. He feared that Bonaparte might over-popularize the corruption under McKinley since Bonaparte as a Harvard overseer had voted against giving McKinley an honorary degree.

49. The best account of the work of Conrad and Bonaparte is found in Eric F. Goldman, *Charles J. Bonaparte, Patrician Reformer* (Baltimore, 1943), pp. 50–65.

50. Bonaparte to Jerome Bonaparte, June 27, 1903, Bonaparte Papers.

51. Bonaparte to Holmes Conrad, July 19, 1904, Bonaparte Papers.

52. Payne to Roosevelt, July 9, 1903, Roosevelt Papers.

53. Bonaparte to Moorfield Storey, Aug. 1, 1903, Bonaparte Papers.

54. Bonaparte to George McAneny, Aug. 3, 1903, Bonaparte Papers. Holmes Conrad wrote to Roosevelt on Oct. 6, 1903, that they could get enough evidence to indict but not enough to prove Heath guilty. Roosevelt Papers. Bristow continued the investigation until early 1904.

55. Charles E. Smith to Roosevelt, June 23, 1903, Roosevelt Papers; Fowler, *The Cabinet Politician*, p. 275. Bonaparte's report on the Tulloch charges to the Attorney General was dated November 11, 1903. See Bonaparte Papers for complete file; also Washington *Post*, Dec. 19, 1903.

56. 58th Cong., 2nd sess., *Senate Doc., Nos. 151–81*, V, 199.

57. William Allen White, "Roosevelt and the Postal Frauds," *McClure's Magazine,* XXIII (May–Oct., 1904), 506–20. Roosevelt acknowledged White's work in his letter of transmission of Bristow's report to Congress.

58. New York *Times*, Jan. 11, Feb. 29, 1904; New York *Nation,* Apr. 30, 1904.

59. Bonaparte to Conrad, Oct. 3, 1904, Bonaparte Papers.

60. New York *Times*, Mar. 7, 1904. Some of the prominent names were Senators Cullom, Beveridge, Carter, Quay, and Penrose and Representatives Wadsworth, Bow-ersock, Lilley, Howell, and Grosvenor.

61. R. T. Wynne to Payne, Mar. 12 and Mar. 14, 1904, Roosevelt Papers. All the material relating to leases and rents for the House of Representatives Report No. 1395 was furnished. See complete memo in Roosevelt Papers on March 16, 1904. Payne to Rep. Jesse Overstreet, Feb. 5, 1904. (Exhibit H), lists offices for which congressmen had sought increases in salaries and rents.

62. 58th Cong., 2nd sess., *House Report, No. 1395;* Fowler, *The Cabinet Politician,* pp. 276–77. See also 58th Cong., 2nd sess., *Congressional Record,* pp. 51, 2932–34, 2961, 3052, 3070, 3116–31.

63. A partial list of the convictions is given by White, "Roosevelt and the Postal Frauds," *McClure's Magazine,* XXIII (May–Oct., 1904) 518–19. See also Washington *Post,* Jan. 8, 1904, and Feb. 8, 1905; Bonaparte to Roosevelt, Sept. 17, 1903. Bonaparte Papers.

64. Washington *Post,* Jan. 24, Nov. 26, 1904, Jan. 18, 1905; Kirke Mechem, ed., *The Annals of Kansas* (Topeka, 1954), I (1886–1910), 427, 442–43, 447.

65. Post Office Department, *Annual Report,* 1905, pp. 33 ff.

66. See Washington *Post,* Jan. 14, 1905.

67. Post Office Department Letter Books, No. 62, Dec. 1, 1904, Jan. 10, 19, 1905. See also Roosevelt to White, Dec. 20, 1904, White Papers, Division of Manuscripts, Library of Congress, Washington.

68. White to Bristow, May 22, 1905, White Papers.

69. Topeka *Journal,* Jan. 19, 1905.

70. White to Thackeray, May 27, 1908, White Papers.

71. Dawes, *A Journal of the McKinley Years,* pp. 405–406.

CHAPTER IV

1. Wynne urged Roosevelt to look into Bristow's tactics as an investigator on the grounds that there were reasons to believe that

Bristow had exceeded the bounds of fairness and humanity. He was accused of being clothed with inquisitorial power and of driving employees to distraction with a big staff of secret service inspectors. Roosevelt ordered an investigation in April, 1905. Congressmen rushed in to blacken Bristow's reputation. See Topeka *Herald,* Mar. 16, 1905. W. E. Cochran, who had been the chief of the post office inspectors, was made purchasing chief at $1,000 increase in salary. Several other effective investigators were transferred to other departments of the federal service.

2. Henry F. Pringle, *The Life and Times of William Howard Taft* (New York, 1939), I, 279–84.

3. *Report of Joseph L. Bristow, Special Panama Railroad Commissioner to the Secretary of War,* June 24, 1905, 59th Cong., 1st sess., *Senate Doc., No. 429.* Bristow reviews his assignment in the beginning of the report. (Hereafter cited as Bristow Report.)

4. Cromwell to Taft, Mar. 8, 1905, Taft Papers, Division of Manuscripts, Library of Congress, Washington.

5. Bristow Report, pp. 10–12.

6. *Ibid.,* pp. 1–10.

7. Salina *Evening Journal,* Mar. 16, 1905.

8. Salina *Evening Journal,* July 11, 1905.

9. Bristow Report, pp. 47 ff.

10. For a description of the work in Panama following the Bristow Report, see especially: George W. Goethals, ed., *The Panama Canal: An Engineering Treatise* (New York, 1916), II, 292–331; Norman J. Padelford, *The Panama Canal in Peace and War* (New York, 1942), pp. 296–300; *Canal Record,* Feb. 26, 1908; *Annual Report of the Isthmian Canal Commission for 1913* (Washington, 1913), p. 48 (on the location of the new road).

11. Washington *Globe Democrat,* Mar. 30, 1908.

12. Long to Taft, June 11, 1905, Taft Papers.

13. The New York *Tribune,* April 11, 1904, had suggested that Bristow should be sent to Washington in Senator Burton's place. Governor Bailey was leaning toward Bristow.

14. For a summary of Burton's case, see Kirke Mechem, ed., *The Annals of Kansas* (Topeka, 1954), 1 (1886–1910), 401, 403, 415, 427, 442, 447, 460.

15. Bristow to Aubrey Harwell, Jan. 22, 1917, Bristow Papers, Archives Division, Kansas State Historical Society, Topeka. Bristow wrote that he had been offered the *Beacon* for $100,000.

16. Wichita *Beacon,* Feb. 28, 1907. In six months Allen was offered $150,000. Later he refused $250,-000. Allen said in 1917 he was afraid to put the price of one-half million on it, for fear he might lose it. Bristow to Harwell, Jan. 22, 1917, Bristow Papers.

17. Ottawa *Evening Herald,* June 19, 20, 1907; Topeka *Capital,* June 21, 1907.

18. Taft to Bristow, Aug. 29, 1907, copy in Taft Papers, original in Bristow Papers.

19. Taft to Bristow, Sept. 4, 1907, copy in Taft Papers, original in Bristow Papers.

20. Wagner to Bristow, Sept. 5, 12, and 19, 1907, Bristow Papers.

21. Bristow to Drake, Sept. 19, 1907, Bristow Papers.

22. Drake to Bristow, Sept. 23, 1907, Bristow Papers.

23. Cahill to Bristow, Sept. 25, 1907, Bristow Papers.

24. Ackerman to Bristow, Dec. 2, 1907, Bristow Papers.

25. The manuscript for this report is in the Bristow Papers. It was published by the Government Printing Office in 1908 with the following title: *Report of J. L. Bristow—Special Railroad Com-*

missioner—On the Advisability of the Establishment of a Pacific Steamship Line by the Isthmian Canal Commission, January 20, 1908. Confidential: To be released when Bristow appears be-

fore the Senate Committee on Interoceanic Canals.

26. White to Lorimer, May 28, 1905, White Papers, Division of Manuscripts, Library of Congress, Washington.

CHAPTER V

1. John D. Bright, ed., *Kansas: The First Century* (New York, 1956), II, 1–9.

2. E. W. Hoch to Cummins, July 29, 1902, and M. J. Sweet to Cummins, Mar. 11, 1904, Cummins Papers, Iowa State Department of History and Archives, Des Moines. Dolliver Papers, State Historical Society of Iowa, Iowa City. Dolliver's most extensive tour was in 1908.

3. Ottawa *Evening Herald,* June 7, 1907.

4. Topeka *Capital,* May 1, 1906.

5. Topeka *Capital,* July 19, 1906.

6. William Allen White, *The Autobiography of William Allen White* (New York, 1946), pp. 352–53.

7. Raymond L. Flory, "Senator Chester I. Long" (Ph.D. dissertation, University of Kansas, 1955), p. 3.

8. Robert M. LaFollette, *Autobiography* (Madison, Wisc., 1913), pp. 578–79; White to Robert M. LaFollette, July 6, 1906, White Papers, Division of Manuscripts, Library of Congress, Washington. Walter Johnson, *William Allen White's America* (New York, 1947), pp. 156–57. See Kansas City *Star,* July 18–20 and Oct. 9, 1906. Bristow invited LaFollette to assist in the 1894 campaign on July 20, 1894.

9. Bristow to Long, Feb. 1, 1906, Long Papers, Archives Division, Kansas State Historical Society, Topeka.

10. White to Bristow, Jan. 17, 1907, White Papers.

11. For Long's position, see Flory, "Senator Chester I. Long," pp. 4–5.

12. Topeka *Capital,* Jan. 29, 1908.

13. White to Long, Feb. 3, 1908, White Papers.

14. Long to Fitzpatrick, Feb. 19, 1908, Long Papers.

15. Bristow to Hartman, July 27, 1908, Bristow Papers, Archives Division, Kansas State Historical Society, Topeka.

16. White to Morrill, May 13, 1908, White Papers.

17. White to C. W. Ryan, May 28, 1908, White Papers.

18. White to LaFollette, July 1, 1908, White Papers.

19. Salina *Journal,* July 9, 1908; Topeka *Capital,* Aug. 16, 1908.

20. Johnson, *William Allen White's America,* pp. 148–69. Senator Nelson W. Aldrich, Republican of Rhode Island, was chairman of the Senate Committee on Finance and was generally regarded as a champion of investment interests. House Speaker Joseph G. Cannon, Republican of Illinois, often used his power to defeat reform legislation.

21. Kansas City *Star,* May 10, 1908.

22. *Ibid.,* May 17, June 22, 1908; Flory, "Senator Chester I. Long," p. 7.

23. Emporia *Gazette,* Aug. 1, 2, 1908; Kansas City *Star,* Aug. 2, 1908.

24. Johnson, *William Allen White's America,* pp. 165–67.

25. Emporia *Gazette,* July 11, 1908; White, *Autobiography,* pp. 196–97.

26. Emporia *Gazette,* July 16–18, 1908.

27. *Ibid.,* July 20, 1908.

28. Iola *Register,* Aug. 3, 1908; Topeka *Capital,* Aug. 3, 1908.

29. Bristow to L. H. Hodge, Aug. 8, 1908, Bristow Papers.
30. Topeka *Capital,* Aug. 5, 1908.
31. Salina *Evening Journal,* Aug. 6, 1908.
32. Bristow Papers. The Topeka *Capital* reported on August 13, 1908, that Bristow had visited seventy-seven counties and delivered some ninety speeches. Bristow's total expenditures were $3,584.28. In comparison, Stubbs's expenditures totaled $3,713.00. It was widely rumored that the Long forces spent over $25,000.00. See Bristow to John E. Benton, Dec. 5, 1908, Bristow Papers.
33. Long to Albaugh, Aug. 11, 1908, Long Papers.
34. See especially Topeka *Capital,* Aug. 8, 1908.
35. An examination of these messages shows that the progressive influence was not limited to the middle class as is often assumed. Bristow tried to answer all the letters and telegrams. He had four stenographers employed in the first four days after the primary.
36. Murlin to Bristow, Aug. 7, 1908, Bristow Papers.
37. Johnston to Bristow, Aug. 17, 1908, Bristow Papers.
38. Bristow to De Graw, Aug. 11, 1908, Bristow Papers.
39. Bristow to Chase, Aug. 7, 1908, Bristow Papers.
40. Bristow to Lindsey, Aug. 11, 1908, Bristow Papers.
41. Bristow to Benton, Dec. 5, 1908, Bristow Papers.
42. Bristow to Quayle and Bristow to McRoberts, Aug. 11, 1908, Bristow Papers.
43. Charles M. Harl to Frank M.

Hitchcock, June 16, 1908, copy in Cummins Papers.
44. White to Cummins, Aug. 6, 1908, Cummins Papers.
45. Mrs. Bullard to Dolliver, Aug. 24, 1908, Dolliver Papers.
46. White to Roosevelt, Aug. 8, 1908, White Papers.
47. Bristow to Campbell, Aug. 11, 1908, Bristow Papers.
48. Campbell to Bristow, Aug. 17, 1908, Bristow Papers.
49. White to Bristow, Aug. 19, 1908, White Papers.
50. William Bristow to Bristow, Nov. 6, 1908, Bristow Papers.
51. Bristow to Capper, Sept. 7 and 15, 1908, Bristow Papers.
52. Bristow to J. H. Stewart, Nov. 7, 1908, Bristow Papers.
53. Mason to Bristow, Nov. 7, 1908, Bristow Papers.
54. Bristow to Ewing Herbert, Nov. 14, 1908, Bristow Papers.
55. Bristow to P. B. Stone, Jan. 15, 1909, Bristow Papers.
56. Cecil Howes to Bristow, Nov. 24, 1908, Bristow Papers.
57. White to Bristow, Jan. 7, 1909, White Papers. See also Feb. 6, 1909.
58. A cousin, Esther L. Stone, of Paris, Kentucky, wrote to ask when she should apply for a position in the Post Office Department; President Murlin of Baker University sought a position in the consular service.
59. Bristow to Taft, Dec. 8 and 28, 1908, Bristow Papers.
60. Dolliver to Bristow, Dec. 29, 1908, Bristow Papers.
61. Salina *Evening Journal,* Jan. 27, 1909; Topeka *Capital,* Jan. 27, 28, 1909.

CHAPTER VI

1. Bristow Papers, Archives Division, Kansas State Historical Society, Topeka. As early as January 7, 1909, William Allen White had written that Taft might be trying to discipline the insurgents. In this letter he urged Bristow to hit the evils of the transportation system. He also suggested that Bristow join the American Academy

of Political Science; the academy's bulletins would be valuable to the new senator. See also White Papers, Division of Manuscripts, Library of Congress, Washington.

2. Washington *Post,* Mar. 4, 1909.
3. Bristow to Harrison, Feb. 4, 1909, Bristow Papers.
4. Bristow to Frank Bristow, Mar. 5, 1909, Bristow Papers.
5. Bristow to J. A. McAphee, Mar. 11, 1909, Bristow Papers.
6. Bristow to Frank Bristow, Mar. 18, 1909, and Bristow to Harold T. Chase, Mar. 27, 1909, Bristow Papers.
7. *Ibid.*
8. *Ibid.*
9. Bristow to Capper, Mar. 26 and Apr. 2, 1908, Bristow Papers. Actually, MacVeagh was an anti-Bryan Democrat and a Chicago banker when he was selected by Taft.
10. Bristow to Frank Bristow, Mar. 5, 1909, Bristow Papers. Room 304 Senate Office Building.
11. Bristow to Henry J. Allen, Feb. 4, 1909, and Bristow to C. C. Hardy, Feb. 8, 1909, Bristow Papers.
12. Bristow to Henry J. Allen, Apr. 24, 1909, Bristow Papers. Interview with Mrs. Fay N. Seaton, Manhattan, Kansas.
13. Bristow to Frank Bristow, Mar. 9 and 15, 1909, Bristow Papers; Registrar of Deeds Books, Saline County Court House, XXIX, 265; XL, 463; LI, 297.
14. Bristow to Aldrich, Mar. 15 and 16, 1909, Bristow Papers.
15. Bristow to Kirtland, Mar. 20, 1909, Bristow Papers.
16. Bristow to Stubbs, Mar. 24, 1909, Bristow Papers.
17. 61st Cong., 1st sess., *Congressional Record,* pp. 121–22. Later committee assignments: 61st Cong., 2nd sess.: chairman of Expenditures in Post Office Department; Claims; Interoceanic Canals; Public Health and National Quarantine; Railroads; Standards, Weights, and Measures; Transportation Routes to Seaboard

(Bristow held the same for the third session). In the 63rd Congress he served on Banking and Currency in both sessions but dropped from Expenditures in the Post Office Department to a place on the regular postal committee. In the third session he was chairman of Cuban Relations Committee.

18. George E. Mowry, *The Era of Theodore Roosevelt* (New York, 1958), pp. 240–49.
19. For specific statements on tariff see the following letters: Bristow to C. W. Bleuler, Apr. 2; Bristow to F. W. Trigg, Apr. 7; Bristow to J. R. Greenless, Apr. 14; Bristow to H. J. Allen, Apr. 24; and Bristow to H. T. Crane, June 3, 1909, in Bristow Papers.
20. 61st Cong., 1st sess., *Congressional Record,* p. 1760; New York *Tribune,* May 6, 1909.
21. Bristow to Frank Bristow, Apr. 10, 1909, Bristow Papers.
22. Bristow to L. H. Hodge, Apr. 5, 1909, Bristow Papers.
23. *Ibid.*
24. Bristow's correspondence contains numerous letters of inquiry and many of the replies; see especially from March 29 to May 20. See also Bristow to MacVeagh, May 17, 1909, and reply May 20 and 21, 1909; N. J. Stone to Beveridge, April 1, 1910, Beveridge Papers, Division of Manuscripts, Library of Congress, Washington. Dolliver Papers, State Historical Society of Iowa, Iowa City, for April and May, 1909. A letter from the Brooke Scranton Lumber Company, April 23, ridicules Aldrich's position, especially on the need for high tariffs to protect labor.
25. Bristow to E. C. Manning, Apr. 23, 1909, Bristow Papers.
26. Bristow to Frank Bristow, Apr. 19, 1909, Bristow Papers.
27. Quoted in Kansas City *Star,* May 9, 1909. The Topeka *Journal,* May 20, 1909, quoted a long article that had been published in

LaFollette's Weekly, on Bristow's attack on the lead industry. For selections of Bristow's speeches on sugar see 61st Cong., 1st sess., *Congressional Record,* pp. 2394—2408 and 2427–45. There are bound copies of his speeches in the Library of the Kansas State Historical Society, Topeka.

28. Bristow to D. A. Valentine, May 14, 1909, Bristow Papers.
29. Bristow to George M. Hull, May 15, 1909, Bristow Papers.
30. Bristow to Fred Jackson, May 15, 1909, Bristow Papers.
31. Bristow to George Innes, May 14, 1909, Bristow Papers.
32. Bristow to Chase, May 22, 1909, Bristow Papers. On May 6, Bristow burst out with an impassioned denunciation of the conservatives' rudeness and demanded his constitutional rights. "I guess I did it with a good deal of vigor—at least that's what the fellows tell me." See Topeka *Capital,* May 6–13, 1909.
33. Bristow to White, June 8, 1909, Bristow Papers.
34. See especially Bristow to H. M. Beck, April 27; Bristow to George M. Hull, May 15; Bristow to Harold Chase, May 23; and Bristow to A. L. Miller, June 1, 1909, Bristow Papers.
35. Bristow to George M. Hull, June 3, 1909, Bristow Papers.

36. Bristow to D. W. Cowden, June 14, 1909, Bristow Papers.
37. Bristow to White, June 8, 1909, Bristow Papers.
38. As early as March 12, 1909, Taft had written William Allen White that he could not side with the liberals and defend his program. See Taft to White, Mar. 12, 1909, in White Papers. For Taft's later defense see the following letters in the Taft Papers, Manuscript Division, Library of Congress, Washington: Taft to Mrs. E. G. McCagg, June 23, 1909; Taft to Edward Colston, June 24, 1909; Taft to Horace Taft, June 27, 1909; Taft to Mrs. Taft, July 11, 12, 1909; Taft to Charles Taft, July 13, 1909; Taft to William D. Foulke, July 15, 1909; Taft to Horace Taft, August 6, 1909.
39. Bristow to Harold Chase, June 10, 1909, Bristow Papers.
40. *Ibid.;* Bristow to F. C. Trigg, June 21, 1909, Bristow Papers.
41. Bristow to H. J. Allen, July 10, 1909; Bristow to F. C. Trigg, July 21, 1909, Bristow Papers.
42. Mowry, *The Era of Theodore Roosevelt,* pp. 246–47; Taft to William D. Foulke, July 15, 1909; Taft to Charles Curtis, Aug. 6, 1909, Taft Papers.
43. Bristow to Cummins, Sept. 20, 1909, Bristow Papers.
44. Undated manuscript in Bristow Papers.

CHAPTER VII

1. Bristow to Joseph Q. Bristow, Nov. 1, 1909, Bristow Papers, Archives Division, Kansas State Historical Society, Topeka.
2. When Frank Bristow graduated from Baker University in 1908, he was selected as a Rhodes scholar, but his poor health kept him from accepting the grant. It was a pleasant surprise to the entire family when the scholarship offer was renewed in January of 1910, and Frank was able to attend Oxford and continue his legal studies. See Topeka *Capital,* Feb. 1, 1910; Bristow to Nelson Case, Feb. 3, 1910; Bristow to Frank Hageman, Feb. 7, 1910, Bristow Papers.
3. Bristow to Henry J. Allen, Sept. 20, 1909, Bristow Papers.
4. Bristow to Edwin M. Bristow, Dec. 5, 1909, and Feb. 1, 1910, Bristow Papers.

5. Bristow to Trigg, Nov. 3, 1909, Bristow Papers.

6. Bristow to P. B. Stone, June 9, 1910; Bristow to H. W. Moffat, Feb. 3, 1910, Bristow Papers.

7. Bristow to D. W. Cowden, June 14, 1909; Bristow to Henry J. Allen, Dec. 10, 1909, Bristow Papers. See Salina *Evening Journal* for Sept. and Oct., 1909, and Nov. 3, 1909.

8. Bristow to Bass, June 4, 1910, Bristow Papers.

9. Bristow to Beveridge, Oct. 4, 1909, Bristow Papers.

10. Reprinted in Salina *Evening Journal,* Jan. 10, 1910.

11. Bristow to Scott, Oct. 6, 1909.

12. Bristow to O. K. Davis, New York *Times* correspondent, Nov. 1, 1909, Bristow Papers.

13. Bristow to Cummins, Sept. 14, 1909, Bristow Papers.

14. Bristow to Fred S. Jackson, Dec. 6 and 15, 1909; Bristow to Henry J. Allen, Dec. 16, 1909, Bristow Papers.

15. As late as December 24, 1909, Bristow was urging William Allen White not to get into a direct controversy with Taft. Bristow Papers.

16. Bristow to J. H. Stewart, June 19, 1911, Bristow Papers; 61st Cong., 1st sess., *Congressional Record,* pp. 4105–6; Kansas City *Star,* July 5, 1909.

17. Senate Joint Resolution 50 introduced in 61st Cong., 2nd sess., *Congressional Record,* p. 105. See also *ibid.,* pp. 1518, 1824–25, and 8454 for Bristow's efforts to get the resolution reported from committee. Bristow to F. S. Jackson, Dec. 15, 1909, Bristow Papers.

18. See especially Bristow to Harold Chase, Mar. 17, 1913, and Bristow to J. H. Stewart, June 11, 1911, Bristow Papers. Roll-call defeat Feb. 28, 1911, by a vote of 54 to 33.

19. Joseph L. Bristow, "The Bristow Amendment: The Inside Story of the Fight for Direct Election of Senators," *Saturday Evening Post,* CLXXXIV (Sept. 30, 1911), 7–8, 52–53; New York *Tribune,* May 14, 1912. See also 62nd Cong., 3rd sess., *Congressional Record,* pp. 106, 124–30, 1923–25.

20. Bristow to White, May 14, 1912, Bristow Papers.

21. New York *Tribune,* May 14, 1912, and June 14, 1914.

22. See Bristow's letters to state political leaders in Feb., 1913, Bristow Papers.

23. See Bristow to Bryan, Mar. 13, 1913, Bristow Papers.

24. Bristow to Roosevelt, Apr. 9, 1913, Bristow Papers.

25. Washington *Post,* Apr. 9, 1913.

26. The New York *Tribune,* June 1, 1913, called attention to Bristow's absence. Bristow to H. J. Haskell, June 24, 1913, Bristow Papers: "I do not want any more quarrels with the administration than is necessary for me to have."

27. Washington *Post,* Feb. 26, 1913.

28. Roosevelt to Bristow, Dec. 6 and 23, 1912, Bristow Papers.

29. Pinchot to Bristow, Dec. 28, 1912, Bristow Papers.

30. See especially 62nd Cong., 3rd sess., *Congressional Record,* pp. 3911–14; 63rd Cong., 2nd sess., *Congressional Record,* pp. 3598, 4336, 5099; New York *Tribune,* Jan. 31, 1913; and Salina *Evening Journal,* Mar. 30, 1914.

31. Bristow to O. K. Davis, Nov. 1, 1909, Bristow Papers.

32. 62nd Cong., 2nd sess., *Congressional Record,* pp. 3172, 2483–96, 6397–6405, 7375.

33. Taft to Horace Taft, Mar. 5, 1910, Taft Papers, Division of Manuscripts, Library of Congress, Washington. See also Taft to William Allen White, Mar. 2, 1909, White Papers, Division of Manuscripts, Library of Congress, Washington.

34. Taft to Nicholas Longworth, July 15, 1910, Taft Papers.

35. George E. Mowry, *The Era of Theodore Roosevelt* (New York, 1958), pp. 261-62.

36. Bristow to L. P. Coblentz, Jan. 31, 1910; Bristow to H. J. Hoover, Mar. 7, 1910; and Bristow to T. C. Carver, Mar. 8, 1910, Bristow Papers.
37. Taft to Nicholas Longworth, July 15, 1910, Taft Papers.
38. Taft to O. T. Bannard, June 11, 1910, Taft Papers.
39. See Dolliver Papers, State Historical Society of Iowa, Iowa City, for Feb. and Mar., 1909.
40. Bristow to G. E. Runnal, Dec. 8, 1909; Bristow to T. G. O'Donnell, July 24, 1911; Bristow to William Allen White, Nov. 30, 1911, Bristow Papers.
41. New York *Tribune*, Aug. 13, 1912; Salina *Evening Journal*, Aug. 12, 1912.
42. Bristow to P. V. Adee, Mar. 1, 1912; Bristow to J. R. Harrison, July 22, 1912, Bristow Papers.
43. Bristow to Arthur Capper, Feb. 2, 1910, Bristow Papers.
44. In 1902, Clarence Cunningham of Idaho had prospected for coal lands in Alaska and had bought claims for his friends. By 1904 he and his thirty-two associates held 5,280 acres of coal lands, for which they later paid the U.S. Treasury $52,800. Their holdings exceeded the amount allowed under a federal law passed in 1904 that would have limited holdings of such a group to 640 acres. Cunningham and his associates stood to profit from plans of the Morgan-Guggenheim syndicate to build railroads and to develop copper claims. See Henry F. Pringle, *The Life and Times of William Howard Taft* (New York, 1939), I, 484-90.
45. Salina *Evening Journal*, Sept. 28, 1909.
46. Bristow to P. A. Lovewell, Dec. 27, 1909, Bristow Papers.
47. Bristow to Henry Allen, Jan. 7, 1910, Bristow Papers.
48. Wallace to Dolliver, Jan. 10, 1910, Dolliver Papers.
49. Salina *Evening Journal*, June 28, 1911; Bristow to Gifford Pinchot, July 6, 1911, Bristow Papers.
50. New York *Tribune*, May 16, 1909.
51. Bristow to Taft, Dec. 8, 1910; Bristow to William Allen White, Dec. 8 and 10, 1909, Bristow Papers.
52. Bristow to Arthur Capper, Dec. 31, 1909, Bristow Papers.
53. Salina *Evening Journal*, Sept. 19, 1910. Charles D. Norton, secretary to Taft, promised the Iowa liberals that the President would act fairly in the patronage. Salina *Evening Journal*, Sept. 10, 1911.
54. Eisenhower to Bristow, Aug. 20, 1910, Bristow Papers.
55. Sterl to Bristow, Aug. 23, 1910, Bristow Papers.
56. Bristow to P. W. Heath, Oct. 26, 1910, Bristow Papers.
57. Bristow to Henry Allen, Feb. 14, 1911, Bristow Papers.
58. Bristow to Ida M. Tarbell, Feb. 2, 1911, Bristow Papers.
59. Kansas City *Star*, June 23, 1911; 62nd Cong., 1st sess., *Congressional Record*, pp. 2907, 2932-39.
60. Bristow to Harrison, June 19, 1911, Bristow Papers.
61. 62nd Cong., 1st sess., *Congressional Record*, pp. 3090, 3160-61; New York *Tribune*, Aug. 12, 1911.
62. Salina *Evening Journal*, Sept. 25, 1911.
63. See Senate Bill S 7970.
64. Bristow to Hemingway, Apr. 18, 1910, Bristow Papers.

CHAPTER VIII

1. Hobart to Dolliver, Nov. 9, 1896, Dolliver Papers, State Historical Society of Iowa, Iowa City.
2. See Dolliver to N. W. Rowell, July 16, 1910, Dolliver Papers.
3. Beveridge to Dolliver, July 13, 1910, Dolliver Papers.
4. Bristow to George M. Hull, Mar.

24, 1910, Bristow Papers, Archives Division, Kansas State Historical Society, Topeka.

5. Bristow to White, June 10, 1910, Bristow Papers.

6. Bristow to Kimball, June 3, 1910, Bristow Papers.

7. Bristow to White, July 2, 1910, Bristow Papers.

8. Beveridge to Bristow, July 14, 1910, Beveridge Papers, Division of Manuscripts, Library of Congress, Washington.

9. Beveridge to Bristow, Aug. 9, 1910, Beveridge Papers.

10. Bristow to Bourne, July 1, 1910, Bristow Papers.

11. Fish to Norris, July 3, 1910, Norris Papers, Division of Manuscripts, Library of Congress, Washington.

12. Bristow to Cummins, July 11, 1910; Bristow to Dolliver, July 12, 1910, Bristow Papers.

13. Bristow to Jones, July 7, 1910, Bristow Papers.

14. Memorandum dated July 7, 1910, Taft Papers, Division of Manuscripts, Library of Congress, Washington.

15. Bristow to Roosevelt, July 15, 1910, Bristow Papers.

16. Salina *Journal,* July 11, 1910.

17. See Beveridge to Bristow, July 14, 1910, Beveridge Papers, on the Winfield speech.

18. Ida Tarbell to Bristow, Aug. 2 and Sept. 15, 1910, Bristow Papers.

19. Kansas City *Star,* July 29, 1910.

20. Bristow to Beveridge, Aug. 18, 1910, Bristow Papers.

21. Bristow to H. J. Haskell, Aug. 6, 1910; Bristow to Dora Kershner, May 25, 1911, Bristow Papers; and Emporia *Gazette,* Aug. 12, 1910.

22. Bristow to Dolliver, July 20, 1910, Dolliver Papers.

23. *Ibid.*

24. Towne to Dolliver, July 20, 1910, Dolliver Papers.

25. Bristow to Gore, Aug. 2, 1910, Bristow Papers.

26. Bristow to Hannan, Aug. 2, 1910, Bristow Papers.

27. Bristow to Cummins, to Beveridge, to Clapp, and to LaFollette, each dated Aug. 3, 1910, Bristow Papers. See especially Bristow to Beveridge, Aug. 5, 1910, for a detailed evaluation of the political issues by Bristow.

28. White to Dolliver, Aug. 9, 1910, Dolliver Papers.

29. Bristow to Nelson, Aug. 5, 1910, Bristow Papers.

30. George L. Mowry, *Theodore Roosevelt and the Progressive Movement* (Madison, Wisc., 1946), pp. 127 ff.; Bristow to Beveridge, Aug. 5, 1910, Bristow Papers. Lincoln Steffens headed a fund-raising drive for LaFollette.

31. Bristow to Beveridge, Aug. 18, 1910, Beveridge Papers.

32. Hannan to Dolliver, Aug. 13, 1910, Dolliver Papers.

33. LaFollette to Beveridge, Sept. 22, 1910, Beveridge Papers.

34. Beveridge to Cummins, Aug. 11, 1910, Beveridge Papers.

35. Salina *Evening Journal,* Sept. 17, 1910.

36. Bristow to Frank Bristow, Sept. 8, 1910; Bristow Papers.

37. Bristow to Ray Stannard Baker, Oct. 25, 1910, Bristow Papers.

38. This estimate was made by Beveridge to Frank Hitchcock on November 22, 1910 (Beveridge Papers). Bristow wrote Moses E. Clapp, November 11, 1910, that if Indiana had had the direct vote, Beveridge would have carried the election by 100,000 votes. Beveridge wrote Bristow listing three factors in his defeat: (1) brewery interests, (2) unlimited money from somewhere, (3) deep resentment over the new tariff and general dissatisfaction with everything. Beveridge to Bristow, Nov. 1, 1910, Beveridge Papers.

39. Bristow to Beveridge, Sept. 26, 1910, Beveridge Papers.

40. Bristow to Baker, Oct. 25, 1910, Bristow Papers.

41. Bristow to Shaw, Nov. 7, 1910, Bristow Papers.

42. Bristow to Frank Bristow, Mar. 15, 1911, Bristow Papers.

43. Bristow to L. C. Magill, Feb. 11, 1911; Bristow to Frank Bristow, May 15, 1911, Bristow Papers.

44. Bristow to Norris Brown, Aug. 29, 1911, Bristow Papers.

45. Bristow to Lucile Brown, June 6, 1912, Bristow Papers.

46. Bristow to Frank Bristow, July 28 and Aug. 16, 1911, Bristow Papers.

47. Bristow to Bourne, Oct. 2, 1911; Bristow to Allen, Oct. 2, 1911, Bristow Papers. Interview with Mrs. Hardy of Washington, D.C.

48. Belle Case and Fola LaFollette, *Robert M. LaFollette* (New York, 1953), pp. 314–22.

49. Bristow to William Youngblood, May 1, 1911, Bristow Papers.

50. Bristow to Roosevelt, May 2, 1911, Bristow Papers.

51. Bristow to George M. Hull, June 16, 1911, Bristow Papers.

52. Bristow to Allen, July 18, 1911, Bristow Papers.

53. Bristow to John Simmons, Apr. 3, 1911, Bristow Papers.

54. Bristow to White, Nov. 30, 1911, and Jan. 11, 1912; Bristow to J. R. Harrison, Feb. 12, 1912, Bristow Papers.

55. Bristow to Taft, June 13, 1911, Bristow Papers.

56. Bristow to Allen, Oct. 6, 1911, Bristow Papers.

57. Bristow to Frank Hageman, Feb. 9, 1912, Bristow Papers. On July 11, Bristow wrote Capper, "I want it distinctly understood in the state that I am for LaFollette." Bristow Papers.

58. Bristow to Chase, Aug. 9, 1911, Bristow Papers.

59. Bristow to Capper, Dec. 26, 1911, Bristow Papers.

60. This idea, expressed by Bristow to Fola LaFollette, July 16, 1937, was contained in Fola LaFollette's "Interview Notes" furnished to the author.

61. Bristow to Harrison, Jan. 2, 1912, Bristow Papers.

62. Bristow to Frank Bristow, Jan. 3, 1912, Bristow Papers.

63. Bristow to C. D. Skimmer, May 27, 1912, Bristow Papers. See material from Fola LaFollette's "Interview Notes." White wrote to Rodney Elard on November 12, 1912, that "Joe told me after the Philadelphia speech he could not conveniently support LaFollette for President since he feared in the presidency LaFollette might have the same type of mental attack." White Papers.

64. Bristow to Quincy, May 24, 1912, Bristow Papers.

65. Bristow to George N. Hull, June 25, 1912, Bristow Papers.

66. *Ibid.*

67. Bristow to Capper, Aug. 1, 1912, Bristow Papers.

68. Bristow to Roosevelt, May 30, 1912, Bristow Papers.

69. See copies of interviews in Bristow Papers.

70. Bristow to Cummins, Oct. 21, 1912, Bristow Papers: "I am speaking twice a day now, and I am having the best meetings that I have ever had in Kansas; but we have a hard fight."

71. For a recent description of the 1912 election in Kansas, see Homer E. Socolofsky, *Arthur Capper, Publisher, Politician and Philanthropist* (Lawrence, Kans., 1962), pp. 74–81.

72. White to Roosevelt, Nov. 14, 1912, White Papers.

73. *Ibid.*

74. Bristow to Lockard, Nov. 26, 1912, Bristow Papers.

75. Beveridge to White, Nov. 18, 1912, Beveridge Papers.

76. Roosevelt to Bristow, Nov. 15, 1912, Bristow Papers.

77. Bristow to W. Y. Morgan, Dec. 12, 1912; Bristow to White, Dec. 5, 1912, Bristow Papers.

CHAPTER IX

1. Washington *Post,* Mar. 4, 1913.
2. For the campaign in 1912 see Arthur S. Link, *Woodrow Wilson and the Progressive Era, 1910-1917* (New York, 1954), pp. 3–24.
3. Bristow to R. A. Burch, Dec. 9, 1912; Bristow to C. D. Slinkers, Dec. 9, 1912; Bristow to Arthur Capper, Dec. 27, 1912, Bristow Papers, Archives Division, Kansas State Historical Society, Topeka.
4. Bristow to G. T. Davies, Feb. 18, 1913, Bristow Papers.
5. Bristow to Dolley, Dec. 16, 1912, Bristow Papers. See also Bristow to Theodore Roosevelt, Dec. 14, 1912, Bristow Papers.
6. Bristow to Solon T. Williams, Sept. 8, 1913, Bristow Papers.
7. Bristow to William Allen White, June 19, 1913, Bristow Papers.
8. Bristow to White, June 12, 1913, Bristow Papers.
9. Bristow to Frank Bristow, Apr. 5, 1913, Bristow Papers.
10. Bristow to H. J. Allen, Sept. 5, 1913, Bristow Papers.
11. Bristow to Arthur Capper, Feb. 5, 1915, Bristow Papers. See Bristow to Fred H. Quincy, June 23, 1913; Link, *Woodrow Wilson and the Progressive Era,* pp. 79–80.
12. New York *Times,* July 16, 1913.
13. *Ibid.,* July 19, 1913.
14. *Ibid.,* July 17, 1913.
15. Bristow to S. S. Reynolds, July 22, 1913, Bristow Papers.
16. Bristow to John Madden, Feb. 21, 1913, Bristow Papers.
17. Bristow to Madden, Mar. 7, 1913, Bristow Papers.
18. 63rd Cong., 1st sess., *Congressional Record,* pp. 4228–29, 5846–47; New York *Times,* Nov. 4, 1913.
19. *Ibid.,* Nov. 3, 1913.
20. Bristow to Valentine, Dec. 13, 1913, Bristow Papers.
21. Bristow to Frank Bristow, Apr. 17, 1914, Bristow Papers.
22. *Ibid.* For more on the Tampico incident see R. E. Quirk, *An Affair of Honor: Woodrow Wilson and the Occupation of Veracruz* (Lexington, Ky., 1962).
23. 63rd Cong., 2nd sess., *Congressional Record,* pp. 697–98.
24. New York *Times,* Apr. 23, 1914.
25. Bristow to Pomeroy, Apr. 23, 1914, Bristow Papers.
26. New York *Times,* Apr. 25, 1914.
27. Salt Lake City *Republican,* Apr. 5, 1915.
28. Bristow to H. J. Allen, Dec. 23, 1914, Bristow Papers.
29. Beveridge to Bobbs, Mar. 22, 1914, Beveridge Papers, Division of Manuscripts, Library of Congress, Washington.
30. Bristow to Ord Clingman, Mar. 13, 1914; Bristow to J. R. Harrison, May 19, 1914, Bristow Papers.
31. New York *Times,* Mar. 31, 1914.
32. Washington *Post,* June 1 and June 9, 1914.
33. New York *Times,* Feb. 19, 1914; Washington *Post,* June 11, 1914.
34. New York *Times,* Feb. 21, 1914. The editor declared that Bristow had forgotten his "standing and dignity." See also New York *Times,* May 8, 1914.
35. Washington *Post,* June 12, 13, 1914.
36. New York *Times,* Oct. 3, 1914; 63rd Cong., 2nd sess., *Congressional Record,* pp. 16056, 16520–21; Salina *Evening Journal,* Mar. 4, 1915.
37. Bristow to Fred Perkins, Apr. 18, 1913, Bristow Papers.
38. Bristow to Theodore Roosevelt, Apr. 17, 1913, Bristow Papers.
39. 63rd Cong., 1st sess., *Congressional Record,* pp. 3467–68, 3513–14, 3725, 4551.
40. *Ibid.,* p. 3772.
41. Bristow to White, May 22, 1913; Bristow to George W. Hanna, May 3, 1913, Bristow Papers.

42. Bristow to H. J. Haskell, Aug. 9, 1913, Bristow Papers.
43. Bristow to Fred Trigg, Dec. 2, 1913, Bristow Papers.
44. Bristow to White, June 27, 1913, Bristow Papers.
45. See especially Bristow to J. M. Walker, July 5, 1913, and Bristow to Harold Chase, July 9 and 31, 1913, Bristow Papers.
46. 63rd Cong., 2nd sess., *Congressional Record*, pp. 520, 1075–78, 1135, 1142; Salina *Evening Journal*, Sept. 24, Nov. 17, 1913.
47. Bristow to Dixon, Nov. 29, 1913, Bristow Papers.
48. 63rd Cong., 2nd sess., *Congressional Record*, pp. 1472–73; New York *Times*, Sept. 30, Oct. 1, Dec. 23, 1913.
49. Bristow to Hitchcock, Dec. 1, 1913, Bristow Papers.
50. New York *Times*, Dec. 23, 1913.
51. Washington *Post*, July 10, Aug. 4, 8, 1914; Link, *Woodrow Wiland the Progressive Era*, pp. 76–78.
52. New York *Times*, Aug. 6, 1914.

Bristow wrote that he had spoken four hours against Warburg during the committee's executive session. Bristow to George I. Wilson, August 8, 1914, Bristow Papers.
53. New York *Times*, Oct. 3, 1914.
54. Quoted in Link, *Woodrow Wilson and the Progressive Era*, p. 74.
55. Bristow to Gilman Carter, Jan. 21, 1914, Bristow Papers.
56. New York *Times*, July 30, 1913.
57. See Senate Bill S 4281. Bristow gave a long speech in the Senate, January 31, 1914, on conservation. See also Bristow to David F. Houston, Mar. 17, 1914, and Bristow to Thomas P. Gore, Apr. 10, 1914, Bristow Papers.
58. Bristow to White, Mar. 19, 1914, Bristow Papers; *The Parcel Post: Report of the Joint Committee to Investigate the General Parcel Post*, 63rd Cong., 3rd sess., *Senate Doc. No. 941*. Presented by Bristow Feb. 12, 1915; Salina *Evening Journal*, Feb. 23, 1915.

CHAPTER X

1. Beveridge to White, July 6, 1914, White Papers, Division of Manuscripts, Library of Congress, Washington.
2. In Beveridge Papers, Division of Manuscripts, Library of Congress, Washington.
3. See especially a letter from White to Mrs. Monrose, Feb. 9, 1914, White Papers.
4. F. W. Dixon to White, Dec. 9, 1912, White Papers.
5. J. B. Brown to White, Dec. 9, 1912, White Papers.
6. M. B. Ingle to White, Nov. 13, 1912, White Papers.
7. Perkins to White, Nov. 13, 1912, White Papers.
8. P. H. Pearson to White, Dec. 9, 1912, White Papers.
9. Bristow to Frank Bristow, Nov. 9, 1912, Bristow Papers, Archives

Division, Kansas State Historical Society, Topeka.
10. Bristow to Beveridge, Dec. 21, 1912, Bristow Papers.
11. Bristow to Harrison, Dec. 21, 1912, Bristow Papers.
12. Bristow to Frank Bristow, Jan. 14, 1913, Bristow Papers.
13. Bristow to Beveridge, Dec. 31, 1912, Bristow Papers.
14. Bristow to Harrison, Feb. 3, 1913; Harrison to Bristow, Sept. 18, 1913, Bristow Papers.
15. Bristow to Sartin, Feb. 7, 1913, Bristow Papers.
16. Bristow to Frank Bristow, Apr. 5, 1913, Bristow Papers.
17. Bristow to Capper, Apr. 5, 1913, Bristow Papers.
18. Emporia *Gazette*, May 22, 1913.
19. Beck to White, Oct. 18, 1913, White Papers.

20. Rankin to White, Dec. 17, 1913, White Papers. Rankin was an employee of Capper Publications, and T. A. McNeal was furnishing some of his political arguments.

21. Cummins debated his position with Moses Clapp on January 20, 1914, in Philadelphia before the American Academy of Political and Social Science.

22. Harrison to Bristow, Sept. 18, 1913, Bristow Papers.

23. Bristow to White, Nov. 3, 1913, Bristow Papers.

24. Bristow to White, Nov. 12, 1913, Bristow Papers.

25. Bristow to Dixon, Nov. 29, 1913, Bristow Papers.

26. Bristow to Allen, Dec. 31, 1913, Bristow Papers.

27. Kansas City *Journal,* Jan. 3, 1914. On January 1, 1914, the Kansas City *Star* carried a full-page article on the Progressive candidate, Murdock.

28. David S. Hinshaw to Beveridge, Jan. 16, 1914, Beveridge Papers. Hinshaw wrote, "Bristow has left us, but from all I can hear from Kansas, his leaving did not in any way weaken us."

29. White to Roosevelt, Feb. 7, 1914, White Papers.

30. See especially Bristow to W. M. Sutton, Jan. 13, 1914; Bristow to O. W. Dawson, Jan. 5, 1914, Bristow Papers.

31. New York *Times,* Jan. 26, 1914.

32. Bristow to Capper, Jan. 22, 1914. Bristow Papers. Bristow thanked Capper for the way the *Capital* had handled his decision. He wrote, "Personally, I do not intend to give any attention to Will White's attacks on me."

33. Bristow to A. L. Cook, July 6, 1914, Bristow Papers. Interview with Bailey, Salina, Kans., May 23, 1961.

34. Bristow to G. H. Buckman, June 5, 1914, Bristow Papers. On July 16, 1914, he wrote to Capper: "I can do nothing else but remain here. . . . So I have concluded to stay and do the best I can, and leave my fortunes with the people."

35. Harrison to Bristow, May 16, 1914, Bristow Papers.

36. Bristow to Morgan, May 23, 1914, Bristow Papers.

37. See especially W. D. Ross to White, Jan. 22, 1914, and E. S. Bower to White, Feb. 3, 1914, White Papers.

38. White to Roosevelt, June 17, 1914, White Papers.

39. White to Murdock, Mar. 7, 1914, White Papers.

40. Perkins to White, Feb. 2, 1914, White Papers.

41. Sartin to White, July 28, 1914, White Papers.

42. Bristow to Bailey, June 10, 1914; Bristow to S. A. Lockwood, May 14, 1914, Bristow Papers.

43. Bristow to Bailey, July 3, 1914, Bristow Papers.

44. Bristow to Harrison, July 9, 1914, Bristow Papers.

45. Bristow to Morton Albaugh, June 6, 1914, Bristow Papers.

46. Bristow to Frank Bristow, June 24, 1914, Bristow Papers.

47. Interview with Roy F. Bailey, Salina, Kans., May 23, 1961.

48. Bristow to Harrison, July 30, 1914, Bristow Papers.

49. Interview with Mrs. Fay N. Seaton, Manhattan, Kans., May 17, 1961.

50. New York *Times,* Aug. 5–7, 1914.

51. Bristow to Amrine, Aug. 6, 1914, Bristow Papers.

52. Bristow to Capper, Aug. 6, 1914, Bristow Papers.

53. Bristow to J. A. Burnette, Aug. 19, 1914, Bristow Papers.

54. Bristow to Jack Harrison, Aug. 12, 1914, Bristow Papers.

55. Bristow to Trigg, Nov. 6, 1914, Bristow Papers.

56. Bailey to White, Nov. 26, 1914, White Papers.

CHAPTER XI

1. Interview with Roy F. Bailey, Salina, Kans., May 23, 1961.
2. Kansas Corporation Charter Books, Number 32, pp. 370–71. Kansas State Historical Society, Topeka.
3. Bristow to Harwell, Jan. 22, 1917, Bristow Papers, Archives Division, Kansas State Historical Society, Topeka. It is interesting to note how Bristow's associates turned to journalism. His chief political adviser, J. R. Harrison, bought the Beloit *Gazette;* Fay Seaton, his first Senate assistant, bought the Manhattan *Mercury;* another member of his clerical staff, C. C. Hardy, went to Lincoln, Kansas, to edit the *Republican.*
4. Kansas Corporation Charter Books, Corp. A. 14B, p. 29.
5. Bristow to Frank Bristow, Aug. 7, 1914, Bristow Papers.
6. Bristow to Moses E. Clapp, Apr. 30, 1915, Bristow Papers.
7. Bristow to S. B. Byrne, Jan. 4 and Apr. 7, 1915; Bristow to F. E. Dawley, Jan. 7, 1915; Dawley to Bristow, Jan. 25, 1915; Bristow to Frank Bristow, Sept. 29, 1914, and Feb. 8, 1915, Bristow Papers. At the Fairfax County fair the Bristow farm took a first ribbon on white corn, a first on a Red Polled bull, and a first on Dorset sheep.
8. *Time* magazine, X (Oct. 31, 1927), 9.
9. Interview with Roy Bailey, Salina, Kans., May 23, 1961.
10. Topeka *Capital,* June 18, 1937. Ossian Hall is now gone. After an unsuccessful attempt to make it into a museum, it was destroyed to make way for new residences. Today its location is indicated by a small marker in Annandale. In 1942, Bristow sold 2,300 acres. A buyer held an option on the remainder of the estate, but the option expired shortly before

Bristow's death in 1944. The Kansas City *Star* reported on July 12, 1951, that a part of the estate was sold as a country club golf course for approximately $1,000,000.
11. White to J. W. Moore, Nov. 20, 1914, White Papers.
12. Bristow to R. A. Harris, Nov. 23, 1914; Bristow to W. L. Huggins, Nov. 23, 1916; Bristow to D. A. Valentine, Nov. 23, 1914, Bristow Papers. Bristow wrote many letters seeking advice.
13. Bristow to Capper, Nov. 28 and Dec. 14, 1914; Bristow to Jonathan Bourne, Jr., Apr. 7, 1915, Bristow Papers.
14. Bristow to Moses Clapp, Apr. 7, 1915, Bristow Papers.
15. Bristow to G. P. McLean, July 16, 1915, Bristow Papers.
16. The I.C.C. rejected this decision. *Fourth Biennial Report of the Public Utilities Commission, State of Kansas* (Dec. 1, 1916–Nov. 30, 1918), pp. 104–38.
17. *Third Biennial Report of the Public Utilities Commission, State of Kansas* (Dec. 1, 1914–Nov. 30, 1916), pp. 6–12.
18. Topeka *Capital,* Jan. 15, 1918.
19. Topeka *Journal,* May 27, June 10, 1918.
20. Bristow to Carl J. Mote, Jan. 31, 1918, Bristow Papers.
21. See *Third Biennial Report,* pp. 43–45.
22. Certified copy to W. S. Allen, Secretary of State, Cummins Papers, Iowa State Department of History and Archives, Des Moines.
23. Bristow to J. J. Moore, July 29, 1915, Bristow Papers.
24. Bristow to Henry Allen, June 18, 1916, Bristow Papers.
25. Bristow to Cummins, Mar. 24, 1916, Bristow Papers.
26. Bristow to J. H. Dixon, Aug. 2, 1916, Bristow Papers.
27. Bristow to Cummins, May 25, 1916, Bristow Papers.

28. Bristow to LaFollette, Sept. 18, 1916, Bristow Papers.
29. See especially Bristow to A. L. Sponsler, Jan. 4, 1915, and Bristow to Roy Buckingham, Dec. 21, 1916, Bristow Papers.
30. New York *Times*, May 9, 1915.
31. Bristow to H. M. Crist, July 14, 1915, Bristow Papers. Bristow wrote to Crist of the Brooklyn *Eagle* that the United States needed forty or fifty submarines, not an army of increased size.
32. Bristow to Moses Clapp, Apr. 11, 1917, Bristow Papers.
33. Bristow to William E. Borah,

June 22, 1917, Bristow Papers.
34. New York *Times*, June 5, 1917.
35. Bristow to White, Jan. 16, 1917, Bristow Papers.
36. Salina *Evening Journal*, May 7, 1918.
37. Salina *Evening Journal*, Aug. 10, 1918.
38. Fola LaFollette's "Interview Notes."
39. Topeka *Capital*, June 8, 1922.
40. John Walton, "Character and Politics—A Portrait of Joseph L. Bristow," *Filson Club Historical Quarterly*, XXXIV (July, 1960), 262.

Bibliography

This study was based largely on the correspondence of the political leaders of the time. The most important source was the Joseph L. Bristow Papers in the Archives of the Kansas State Historical Society, Topeka. This extensive collection of some fifty-five thousand items has little material for the early years of Bristow's career, but is most valuable for writing the story of midwestern progressivism after 1906. Bristow corresponded with many influential insurgent leaders on almost every issue that arose during his political career. And fortunately for the student, Bristow kept carbon copies of most of his letters. The correspondence with his family gives some of the best personal reflections on political issues, as well as an introduction to the problems which confronted an editor of a midwestern newspaper. The collection is indispensible for the complete story of the political upheaval that struck Kansas at the turn of the century.

Three other collections at the Kansas State Historical Society contained useful material. The Papers of the Kansas Governors are valuable for political issues. The Arthur Capper Papers, a very extensive collection, offers many letters on the economic and political conditions in the nation. Capper's letters to Republican party leaders were valuable for the study of Bristow. The Chester I. Long Papers, used to supplement the Bristow study from 1900 to 1908, brings out the issues which split the Republican party in Kansas.

Two collections in Iowa, the Albert B. Cummins Papers in the Iowa State Department of History and Archives, Des Moines, and the Jonathan P. Dolliver Papers in the State Historical Society of Iowa, Iowa City, are essential for the story of liberalism in the Midwest. Unfortunately, the Cummins collection is far from complete for the period after Bristow entered the Senate. Both collections have letters from Bristow, William Allen White, and other political leaders in Kansas.

Several of the collections in the Manuscript Division of the Library of Congress, Washington, were used for this study. The

Albert J. Beveridge Papers has the largest number of letters from progressive leaders of the time. Beveridge's own letters present the ideals and goals sought by the progressives. The William Allen White Papers are of special value, not only for the letters to and from prominent national figures, but also for the problems encountered in the organizing and financing of a third-party campaign. The Theodore Roosevelt Papers touch on almost every economic and social issue and are especially valuable for the story of the liberal Republican revolt. The William Howard Taft Papers bring out the political feuds and are the best for the national issues during his Presidency. The early George Norris Papers present a clear picture of the progressive struggle in the House of Representatives. The Woodrow Wilson Papers contain some letters from those supporting the later progressive movement. Two collections by leaders of the movement for civil service reform, the Charles J. Bonaparte and the William D. Foulke Papers, are best for the story of the reform of patronage abuses. The Postal Letter Books in the National Archives were essential for the study of the postal scandals described in Chapter III.

The most valuable newspapers for this study were the New York *Times,* the Washington *Post,* the Kansas City *Star,* and the Topeka *Capital.* The Kansas City *Star* was very sympathetic to liberal issues. Bristow's own publications, the Salina *Evening Journal* and the *Irrigation Farmer* were basic to this study. Many other local and national newspapers and periodicals are cited in the footnotes.

Many books written on this period of history were used and cited in the footnotes. Two books on Kansas history, William F. Zornow, *Kansas: A History of the Jayhawk State* (Norman, Okla., 1957) and John D. Bright, ed., *Kansas: The First Century,* 2 vols. (New York, 1956), kept the local political events in order. For the broader national picture the following works are valuable and necessary: Margaret Leech, *In the Days of McKinley* (New York, 1959); George E. Mowry, *The Era of Theodore Roosevelt* (New York, 1958); Arthur S. Link, *Woodrow Wilson and the Progressive Era* (New York, 1954); Walter Johnson, *William*